The Concise
Company Fi
its Manag

The Concise Guide to Company Finance and its Management

R.E. Brayshaw

Senior Lecturer
Department of Accounting and Finance
University of Birmingham

CHAPMAN & HALL

University and Professional Division

London · New York · Tokyo · Melbourne · Madras

Published by Chapman & Hall, 2–6 Boundary Row, London SE1 8HN

Chapman & Hall, 2–6 Boundary Row, London SE1 8HN, UK

Chapman & Hall, 29 West 35th Street, New York NY10001, USA

Chapman & Hall Japan, Thomson Publishing Japan, Hirakawacho Nemoto Building, 7F, 1-7-11 Hirakawa-cho, Chiyoda-ku, Tokyo 102, Japan

Chapman & Hall Australia, Thomas Nelson Australia, 102 Dodds Street, South Melbourne, Victoria 3205, Australia

Chapman & Hall India, R. Seshadri, 32 Second Main Road, CIT East, Madras 600 035, India

First edition 1992

© 1992 Chapman & Hall

Typeset in 10/11 pt Palatino by Best-set Typesetter Ltd, Hong Kong
Printed and bound in Hong Kong

ISBN 0 412 35780 1

A catalogue record for this book is available from the British Library

Library of Congress Cataloging-in-Publication data
Brayshaw, R.E.
    The concise guide to company finance and its management/R.E.
Brayshaw. — 1st ed.
        p.   cm.
    Includes bibliographical references and index.
    1. Corporations—Finance.   I. Title.
HG4026.B666   1992
658.15—dc20   91–26314
                                                                CIP

Contents

Preface

This book sets out in a clear and succinct style the techniques, theories and institutional infrastructure of contemporary financial decision making and management. Many finance texts which give comprehensive coverage are somewhat daunting to students because of their size and in some cases the level of mathematical and statistical knowledge assumed. *The Concise Guide to Company Finance and its Management* differs from these in that although being comprehensive in approach it seeks to summarize the techniques and theories of finance so that they can be easily understood by both specialist and non-specialist students of finance. Business men will also find the book useful as a source of reference giving understandable and concise explanations of both the theory and practice of finance.

The book uses many worked examples and illustrations to explain key areas of finance and these coupled with the clear text should enable students to gain a full understanding of the topic under examination.

The book can be used as a first text on undergraduate and MBA programmes and could also be used in conjunction with other texts. Students studying for professional accounting examinations will find the text ideal for revision purposes supplying information in a clear and concise manner.

I should like to thank my Editor, Alan Nelson of the publishers, for his support and patience during the writing of this book. My thanks also go to Karen Hanson and Cynthia Franklin for their excellent word processing skills. Finally my thanks go to the many past students who have used this material and helped to shape the structure and content of this book.

R.E. Brayshaw

1 Financial environment

Introduction

Modern financial theory is based on the assumption that decisions are taken within firms to promote the welfare of the owners. In terms of companies it is assumed that managers seek to maximize shareholders' wealth. However, decisions within companies are taken by managers who are not always involved in ownership. It is possible that managers' objectives could differ from those of shareholders. In addition, in a wider context, the preferences of other groups connected with the firm could be taken into account. The objectives of at least five groups might be considered: the managers themselves, the firm's owners (shareholders), the owners plus all people holding financial claims issued by the firm, all parties involved in the firm's operations, including workers and the firm's customers, and finally society as a whole. Under classical capitalism, maximum social welfare is assumed to be achieved through private ownership of firms which are operated to benefit the owners. However, many people in capitalist societies believe that the managers of large firms should be directly concerned with the welfare of society, not merely the owners or other participants in the firm. Although these broader issues are clearly outside the scope of finance they help to illustrate the constraints within which firms operate.

If it is assumed that management is to act in the best interest of the owners, what criteria should they adopt in making financial decisions? Two possible criteria could be considered — profit maximization or wealth maximization.

Profit maximization

Profit maximization can be criticized in that it does not provide an operationally feasible measure for ranking alternative courses of action in terms of their economic efficiency, except under very limited assumptions. It has three main drawbacks:

1. It is a vague term and can give rise to ambiguity. For example, should we seek to maximize short-run or long-run profits? The rate of profit

or the amount? Profits related to total capital or shareholders' funds only? Residual profits after allowing for normal interest and dividends on capital provided? How should profits be measured for this purpose?

2. An important objection to profit maximization is that it cannot distinguish between two courses of action which provide benefits differing with respect to their timing.

3. Perhaps most significantly, profit maximization ignores the quality of the expected benefits. With risk and uncertainty, neither the amounts nor the rate of profitability provide a basis for selecting projects for adoption.

Wealth maximization

Measuring the net present value of projects provides a single measure which overcomes these difficulties. Costs and benefits of alternative courses of action arising over a number of years can be discounted by an appropriate factor to allow for both the time value of money and risk to arrive at the increase in shareholder wealth expected to accrue from following a particular line of action. This objective is a cornerstone of modern financial theory.

The objective of shareholder wealth maximization, although being clearly in the interest of owners of firms, could conflict with the personal objectives of firms' managers and indeed society as a whole. Supporters of wealth maximization claim that it also maximizes the value of economic output available from a given level of input, measured at prices prevailing in the market. Thus it is a necessary condition for maximizing economic welfare for society as a whole. The argument is similar to that which underlies the 'invisible hand' in the classical economic system. The assumption is that all transactions are carried out through free and efficient markets. However, problems can arise even in free market economies where control of wages or prices may be introduced as a short- or medium-term government policy.

Management objectives

These may diverge from that of shareholder wealth maximization for a number of reasons. Management may seek to maximize sales, profit growth or market share. Their level of remuneration may be linked to some or all of these indicators. Mere survival and peace of mind could also figure in their list of objectives. The latter could lead management towards a policy which sought to satisfy shareholders rather than maximize their welfare.

Managers can be viewed as agents of the owners hired to operate the firm for the owners' benefit. If the firm is owned and managed by the same person, there is no possible conflict in objectives. However, this is one extreme case and in larger organizations management may have little or no share of the ownership. If we assume that managers operate to serve their own best interests then will this coincide with those of the owners? To the extent that there is a divergence in interests, the owners are less well off than they would be if no divergence existed. The owners' losses are costs of the agency relationship. Incentives can be awarded to managers to maximize shareholders' interests. For example rewards could be given in the form of share options exercisable at some future date thus encouraging share price maximization. This would also encourage longer term horizons in planning rather than focussing on short-term profit maximization. There has in fact been much criticism of the 'short-termism' which some writers say leads British companies to concentrate on short-term profitability at the expense of long-term growth. Sometimes the blame has been placed on managers in companies sometimes on those managing investments. If share markets were perfect there would be no problem as share prices would reflect at any time the present value of all future activities of the company. However, in an imperfect and uncertain world this information is just not available and investors will use current information and accounting information relating to past periods. Managers within companies may thus be encouraged to favour activities having an immediate or early impact on reported profits, while investment managers may be encouraged to favour those companies showing high increases in earnings in the short term as this may be seen as an indication of long-term growth. It is also said that investment managers themselves are judged on short-run performance of the portfolios they manage and are therefore under pressure to 'pick winners'. When pressed both company managers and investment managers deny short-termism and claim that long-term growth is their goal! However, the criticism persists and when UK performance is compared with some of our overseas competitors there does still seem to be a case to answer.

The effects of the separation of ownership by shareholders and control by professional managers has been the subject of comment for a considerable number of years. The implicit hypothesis here is that the greater the dispersion of shares among the owners of a company the easier it is for management to ignore the shareholders' wishes and pursue instead motives and goals of their own. However, in the past 20 years there has been a significant change in the pattern of share ownership. Financial institutions now control more than 60% of the issued capital of quoted companies and can therefore be said to have effective control of these companies. This is at the expense of private shareholders who for a considerable number of years have been net sellers of equity holdings. This growth in institutional investment is linked to the taxation and portfolio advantages gained through investing through these intermediaries. Instead of dealing with comparatively small shareholders widely spread throughout the country companies now find that their ownership is becoming more and more concentrated in the hands of large sophisticated investors. It therefore becomes more difficult for managers to ignore the wishes of such shareholders, although any influence is likely to be exerted privately rather than overtly. This trend is expected to continue; although in recent years there have been attempts to encourage wider share ownership this has led to more people owning one or two small investments in privatized companies without significantly changing overall ownership structure.

Taxation

It is necessary to consider taxation as it has far-reaching economic consequences for companies and their shareholders. Although we deal mainly with company taxation it is also necessary to consider the shareholders' tax position, and the main personal taxes together with their potential impact on corporate decision-making are outlined below.

Many financial theories are derived under a set of restrictive assumptions, one of which usually assumes a taxless world. However, in evaluating the relevance of these theories in real-world conditions the existence of tax must be acknowledged and its likely impact evaluated.

Taxation, both corporate and personal, has been criticized as leading to distortions in both project and financial investment. A 100% first-year allowance (FYA) on plant and machinery encouraged the acquisition of capital assets by business. For individuals deductability of pension fund contributions coupled with tax exemption of pension fund income and relief on life insurance premiums has led to personal savings being concentrated in these areas with direct investment in equity suffering. The problem was compounded by high rates of marginal tax as the value of the relief is the allowance multiplied by the rate of tax saved. In the last ten years there have been moves to neutralize the impact of taxation. The 100% FYA was phased out and replaced by annual allowances of 25% on the reducing balance basis; combined with this was a reduction of rates of corporation tax, while in 1984 relief on premiums on new life insurance policies was withdrawn.

Corporate taxation

Corporation tax is paid by companies on their profits and capital gains. The technical rules relating to computation of both of these are complicated and constantly changing. The book states the position at time of writing but the reader should check on the current rules and rates of taxes.

The system of corporation tax can be an important determinant of company decisions. From 1965 to 1973 a classical system was in force in the UK whereby company profits and distributions were taxed separately with no interconnection. This contrasts with the present imputation system introduced in 1973 where the company pays advanced corporation tax (ACT) when making a distribution. The ACT is set off against the company's mainstream corporation tax liability while the same ACT is imputed to shareholders' dividends and covers their liability to basic rate income tax. (The USA has a classical system of company taxation and this should be remembered when considering theoretical and empirical work undertaken in the USA, particularly in respect of financing and dividend decisions).

A comparison of the two systems of corporation tax is shown below:

	Classical system £	Imputation system £
Company profits, before tax	100 000	100 000
Less: corporation tax	35 000	35 000
Profits after tax	65 000	65 000
Less: dividends	32 000	24 000
Retained profits	33 000	41 000

Notes:

		Classical	Imputation
1.	Rates of corporation tax	35%	35%
2.	Basic rate of income tax	25%	25%
3.	Rate of advance corporation tax	—	25/75

Dividend payment: Under the classical system a gross dividend of £32 000 will be declared. Income tax at the basic rate will be deducted by the company when paying the dividend and remitted to the Inland Revenue. Thus the shareholders will receive £24 000 (£32 000 less £8000 remitted to the Inland Revenue) in cash. Their income for tax purposes will be £32 000 and they will be entitled to a tax credit of £8000.

Under the imputation system a dividend of £24 000 will be declared which is wholly payable to the shareholders. At the time of paying the dividend the company must pay to the Inland Revenue advance corporation tax, in this case 25/75 × £24 000 = £8000. The shareholders will receive £24 000 in cash. For income tax purposes they will be regarded as having gross income of £32 000 and will be entitled to a tax credit of £8000.

Non-corporate taxation

Non-corporate taxes include

1. income tax;
2. capital gains tax;
3. inheritance tax;
4. social security contributions;
5. taxes on goods and services (VAT and customs and excise duties);
6. business rates and community charge.

All these taxes will have economic consequences for business managers: (4) will affect the total wage bill while (5) and (6) will affect business costs to the extent that they cannot be passed on to consumers. Taxes (1), (2) and (3) will be of most significance to personal investors, and corporate managers will need to consider the effects of their decisions on shareholders' liability to these taxes.

Income tax is payable by individuals on income, as defined for tax purposes, on a progressive scale with a current maximum rate of 40%. Main deductible exemptions are for interest for house purchase and pension fund contributions.

Capital gains tax is payable by individuals on realized gains at their marginal rate of income tax. There is an annual exemption (£5500 of gains) at time of writing. Previously marginal rates of income tax were usually higher than CGT, therefore pressure existed to take increases in wealth as capital gains rather than income. This no longer applies either in the UK or the USA and care must be taken in evaluating theories derived and research undertaken under previous tax regimes.

2 Defining the project and methods of appraisal

Introduction

Project appraisal is concerned with identifying, defining and evaluating long-term investment opportunities. Within any dynamic organization this should be a constant process of search and evaluation. It may take many forms and consist of investment aimed at reduction of existing production costs without adding to the production capacity of the business, or investment in new plant with the aim of increasing capacity and sales or acquisition (takeover) of an existing entity with a view to incorporating it into our own organization's activities. All investments, whatever their scale, have the same basic objective; a sacrifice of cash (investment) now with the expectation of increased cash returns in the future.

It should be emphasized at the outset that although some form of quantitative analysis can be an important input into the decision-making process it does not make the decision maker(s) redundant! There may be qualitative factors which cannot be quantified which have to be considered before a final decision is made. Experience, understanding the markets the organization is operating in and common sense are qualities which will always be important in reaching sensible decisions. However, prior analysis can inform decision makers of those projects which should make money and help distinguish between projects competing for valuable resources within the company.

Defining costs and benefits

Initially a project or projects will be identified which are in line with the organization's strategic plan. It is then necessary to prepare forecasts of the costs and benefits associated with each project. This is an important and often neglected part of the project analysis process. As by their nature projects are likely to run for several years, there is a major forecasting exercise to be undertaken before any evaluation technique can be applied. This should involve a realistic assessment of the initial costs and annual benefits to be derived from the project.

Attention should be focussed on **incremental** costs and benefits associated with the project. As the main techniques involve the use of **cash flows** we will concentrate on incremental cash flows in our discussion. The project analyst should ascertain the extra payments and receipts brought about by the adoption of the project; this would include any likely changes in the cash flows of other activities on the adoption of the new project. For example if a new product is likely to hit the sales of an existing product this will have to be considered.

Opportunity costs must also be considered. These occur when resources are committed to a project and those resources have an alternative use and value to the business. For example if a company is to use a factory which could otherwise be sold then the potential sale price would be the opportunity cost of using the factory in the project. Note that it is current use and value which are relevant and not past costs which are irrelevant and known as **sunk** costs. Project analysis is forward looking and considers current and future costs and benefits. Historic costs are meaningless in this type of analysis.

Taxation can be significant in project analysis and any impact of taxation on cash flows must be brought in. In cash flow terms this will be any extra tax payable or tax saved (e.g. because of allowances) as a result of undertaking the project. Changing price levels (inflation) can also be an important factor in projects which are spread over many future years. The treatment of inflation is discussed in Chapter 4.

Methods of project appraisal

Having discussed relevant costs we turn now to techniques of project/investment appraisal. These can be divided into

1. Discounted cash flow (DCF) methods which are based on the cost of borrowing and take interest and time into consideration. These are **Net Present Value** (NPV) and **Internal Rate of Return** (IRR). IRR is also known as **Yield** method.
2. Non-discounting methods which are simpler, easier to understand and sometimes favoured by businessmen. These are **payback** and **Accounting Rate of Return** (ARR).

DCF methods

All DCF methods are based on the principle of compound interest. Suppose we invest £1000 in the bank for two years with interest payable each year of 10% which is not paid out but reinvested.

After one year we would have £1100:

Initial investment		1000
Interest at 10% − Year 1		100
		1100
do.	Year 2	110
and after two years		£1210

This result could also be written as an equation:

$$\text{After one year, value} = 1000\,(1 + 0.1) = \underline{£1100}$$
$$\text{After two years, value} = 1000\,(1 + 0.1)^2 = \underline{£1210}$$

These are terminal values, the end values resulting from our investment. Present value (PV) states the value now of sums to be received in the future. If £1000 invested now becomes £1210 in two years' time with an interest rate of 10%, it follows that £1210 to be received in two years' time has a present value of £1000 to us now if 10% is our opportunity cost of money.

$$\text{PV of £1210 receivable in two years' time} = \frac{1210}{(1 + 0.1)^2} = 1000$$

We can write this as

$$1210\left[\frac{1}{(1 + 0.1)^2}\right]$$

The term in brackets is the two year discount factor at 10% and is the present value of £1 to be received in two years' time assuming an interest rate of 10%.

Tables of discount factors for different interest rates and lengths of time are available and Table 1.1 on page 10 gives details of some discount factors.

Suppose we are faced with an investment requiring an investment of £7000 now which gives incremental cash returns of £3000 for the next three years. Should we accept the investment if we could otherwise invest at the rate of 10% per annum?

$$\begin{aligned}
\text{Net Present Value (NPV)} &= -7000 + \frac{3000}{1 + 0.1} + \frac{3000}{(1 + 0.1)^2} + \frac{3000}{(1 + 0.1)^3}\\
&= -7000 + 3000\,(0.9091) + 3000\,(0.8264)\\
&\quad + 3000\,(0.7513)\\
&= \underline{+460.4}
\end{aligned}$$

In the computation we have used discount factors from Table 1.1. The investment has an NPV of £460.4, indicating that our wealth would be increased by this amount on adoption of the project. On this basis the project should be adopted. The NPV above can in fact be calculated using annuity tables (Table 1.2). An annuity is an annual payment of the same amount and Table 2 gives the present value of annuities of £1 to be received each year for varying periods of time assuming different rates of interest. We can use the three year annuity at 10% to calculate the NPV as follows:

$$\begin{aligned}
\text{NPV} &= -7000 + 3000\,(2.4869)\\
&= \underline{+460.7}
\end{aligned}$$

There is a slight difference due to rounding of the final place of decimals. The annuity factor can in fact be seen to be the sum of the discount factors

Table 1.1 Present value of 1 at compound interest: $(1 + r)^{-n}$

Years (n)	Interest rates (r)										(n)
	6	7	8	9	10	11	12	13	14	15	
1	0.9434	0.9346	0.9259	0.9174	0.9091	0.9009	0.8929	0.8850	0.8772	0.8696	1
2	0.8900	0.8734	0.8573	0.8417	0.8264	0.8116	0.7972	0.7831	0.7695	0.7561	2
3	0.8396	0.8163	0.7938	0.7722	0.7513	0.7312	0.7118	0.6931	0.6750	0.6575	3
4	0.7921	0.7629	0.7350	0.7084	0.6830	0.6587	0.6355	0.6133	0.5921	0.5718	4
5	0.7473	0.7130	0.6806	0.6499	0.6209	0.5935	0.5674	0.5428	0.5194	0.4972	5
6	0.7050	0.6663	0.6302	0.5963	0.5645	0.5346	0.5066	0.4803	0.4556	0.4323	6
7	0.6651	0.6227	0.5835	0.5470	0.5132	0.4817	0.4523	0.4251	0.3996	0.3759	7
8	0.6274	0.5820	0.5403	0.5019	0.4665	0.4339	0.4039	0.3762	0.3506	0.3269	8
9	0.5919	0.5439	0.5002	0.4604	0.4241	0.3909	0.3606	0.3329	0.3075	0.2843	9
10	0.5584	0.5083	0.4632	0.4224	0.3855	0.3522	0.3220	0.2946	0.2697	0.2472	10
11	0.5268	0.4751	0.4289	0.3875	0.3505	0.3173	0.2875	0.2607	0.2366	0.2149	11
12	0.4970	0.4440	0.3971	0.3555	0.3186	0.2858	0.2567	0.2307	0.2076	0.1869	12
13	0.4688	0.4150	0.3677	0.3262	0.2897	0.2575	0.2292	0.2042	0.1821	0.1625	13
14	0.4423	0.3878	0.3405	0.2992	0.2633	0.2320	0.2046	0.1807	0.1597	0.1413	14
15	0.4173	0.3624	0.3152	0.2745	0.2394	0.2090	0.1827	0.1599	0.1401	0.1229	15

Table 1.2 Present value of an annuity of 1: $\dfrac{1 - (1 + r)^{-n}}{r}$

Years (n)	Interest rates (r)									
	6	7	8	9	10	11	12	13	14	15
1	0.9434	0.9346	0.9259	0.9174	0.9091	0.9009	0.8929	0.8850	0.8772	0.8696
2	1.8334	1.8080	1.7833	1.7591	1.7355	1.7125	1.6901	1.6681	1.6467	1.6257
3	2.6730	2.6243	2.5771	2.5313	2.4869	2.4437	2.4018	2.3612	2.3216	2.2832
4	3.4651	3.3872	3.3121	3.2397	3.1699	3.1024	3.0373	2.9745	2.9137	2.8550
5	4.2124	4.1002	3.9927	3.8897	3.7908	3.6959	3.6048	3.5172	3.4331	3.3522
6	4.9173	4.7665	4.6229	4.4859	4.3553	4.2305	4.1114	3.9975	3.8887	3.7845
7	5.5824	5.3893	5.2064	5.0330	4.8684	4.7122	4.5638	4.4226	4.2883	4.1604
8	6.2098	5.9713	5.7466	5.5348	5.3349	5.1461	4.9676	4.7988	4.6389	4.4873
9	6.8017	6.5152	6.2469	5.9952	5.7590	5.5370	5.3282	5.1317	4.9464	4.7716
10	7.3601	7.0236	6.7101	6.4177	6.1446	5.8892	5.6502	5.4262	5.2161	5.0188
11	7.8869	7.4987	7.1390	6.8052	6.4951	6.2065	5.9377	5.6869	5.4527	5.2337
12	8.3838	7.9427	7.5361	7.1607	6.8137	6.4924	6.1944	5.9176	5.6603	5.4206
13	8.8527	8.3577	7.9038	7.4869	7.1034	6.7499	6.4235	6.1218	5.8424	5.5831
14	9.2950	8.7455	8.2442	7.7862	7.3667	6.9819	6.6282	6.3025	6.0021	5.7245
15	9.7122	9.1079	8.5595	8.0607	7.6061	7.1909	6.8109	6.4624	6.1422	5.8474

for the three separate years used in the first calculation. The judicious use of annuity factors can reduce computation time.

In our project appraisal we calculated the NPV by computing the present value of amounts to be received in the future and deducting the initial cost of investment. Another method of project appraisal is to compute the internal rate of return (IRR) or yield of the cash flows. The IRR is the rate of interest at which NPV is equal to zero and represents the maximum rate of interest that could be paid on a loan to finance the initial outlay. Unless microcomputing facilities are available or a calculator with the appropriate functions, IRR has to be calculated by an approximate method. We will illustrate this 'trial-and-error' method using the data relating to the previous example. The method involves finding the rate of interest at which the project has a small positive NPV, then the rate at which it has a small negative NPV and then interpolating between the two rates to find the approximate IRR.

$$\text{NPV of project at } 13\% = -7000 + 3000 \ (2.3612)$$
$$= +83.6$$
$$\text{NPV of project at } 14\% = -7000 + 3000 \ (2.3216)$$
$$= -35.2$$
$$\text{IRR by interpolation} = 13 + \frac{83.6}{83.6 + 35.2} \times 1\%$$
$$= 13.70\%$$

This in fact is an accurate result confirmed by calculator and can be illustrated by the graph in Fig. 2.1. We can therefore appraise projects using either NPV or IRR. The two methods can be summarized as follows.

If an initial outlay K is invested to give a stream of returns S_t in future years where the discount rate is $100r\%$ then,

$$\text{NPV} = \sum_{t=1}^{n} S_t(1 + r)^{-t} - K$$

If $100i\%$ is the IRR, then,

$$\sum_{t=1}^{n} S_t(1 + i)^{-t} - K = 0$$

Projects with positive NPVs should be accepted as should projects with IRRs greater than the company's cost of capital.

A special case of the annuity referred to earlier is the perpetual annuity and the value of a perpetual annuity, or perpetuity as it is usually called, is given by dividing the annual amount by the rate of interest.

Example
What is the present value of £1000 to be received each year in perpetuity if the required rate of return is $12\frac{1}{2}\%$?
    Answer:

$$\text{Present value} = \frac{1000}{0.125}$$
$$= £8000$$

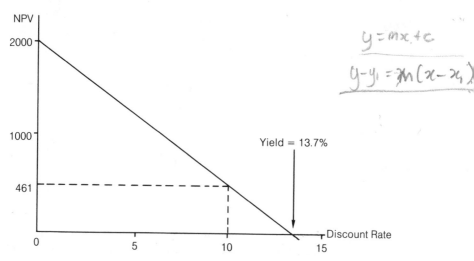

Fig. 2.1. IRR is interest (discount) rate at which NPV is zero.

Non-discounting methods of project appraisal

Payback
This appraises projects by measuring how long it takes to get back the original investment.

Suppose we initially invest £12 000 to give cash flows of £4000 in each of the next five years. The payback period would be three years (3 × £4000 = £12 000). This payback period would then be compared with the company's previously determined minimum payback period.

Accounting Rate of Return (ARR)
Unlike the previous methods of project appraisal examined, ARR uses accounting numbers rather than cash flows. The average accounting profit after charging depreciation is expressed as a percentage of average capital employed invested in the project.

Let us calculate an ARR for the project discussed above under payback. We will assume that depreciation is charged on the initial investment on the straight-line basis over the life of the project and that there is no residual value at the end of the project. This will give depreciation of 12 000/5 = £2400 each year.

The accounting profit each year is calculated as

Annual cash flow	4000	
Less: depreciation	2400	
	£1600	

The average profit is obviously £1600 also in this case. If profits varied from year to year then the total profits would be summed and divided by the life of the project in years (see next chapter for further example).

The average capital employed will be half the initial investment or

12 000/2 = £6000. This will be the usual case where the value of the asset is fully exhausted over the life of the project. If there was a residual value then this would have to be deducted from the initial investment in calculating the average investment. In this case,

$$\text{ARR} = \frac{1600}{6000} \times 100$$
$$= 26.67\%$$

The ARR computed could then be compared with the company return currently being earned or with a predetermined target rate.

Conclusions

In this chapter different methods of project appraisal have been explained. In the next chapter we compare the alternative approaches and comment on the advantages and disadvantages of each.

3 Decision making in project appraisal

Introduction

The basic decision rules relating to the use of each of the techniques introduced in the previous chapter are

Outcome	Decision
NPV > 0	Accept
NPV < 0	Reject
NPV = 0	Indeterminate

Outcome	Decision
IRR > Company cost of capital	Accept
IRR < do.	Reject
IRR = do.	Indeterminate

Payback — accept project if payback period equal to or less than predetermined minimum period; reject project if payback period greater than predetermined minimum period.

Accounting Rate of Return (ARR) — Accept project where average rate of return equal to or greater than predetermined hurdle rate; reject project where average rate of return less than predetermined hurdle rate.

In most cases use of either NPV or IRR will give the decision maker optimal advice in simple accept/reject decisions. However, even with the simplest decisions it is possible for suboptimal and conflicting advice to be given by payback and ARR which if taken could lead to the adoption of loss-making projects and the rejection of wealth-creating projects.

Example

The Z Company Limited has established several procedures for appraising capital expenditure proposals. These procedures require a proposal to meet three tests set out below before it will be further considered.

A proposal to purchase a new milling machine is to be screened. The new machine will cost £11 000 and has an estimated useful life of five years at the end of which the disposal value will just cover the cost of removal. Sales revenue to be generated by the new machine is estimated as follows:

	£
Year 1	6600
Year 2	7200
Year 3	7800
Year 4	8000
Year 5	8000

Additional operating costs are estimated to be £3200 per annum. Tax rates may be assumed to be 50%, payable in the year in which revenue is received. For taxation purposes the machine may be written off at a fixed annual rate of 20% of cost. The statutory financial statements issued by the company show that in recent years profits after tax have averaged 18% on total assets as shown in the balance sheet.

The screening criteria established by the management are as follows:

1. No project should involve a net commitment of funds for more than four years.
2. Accepted proposals must offer a time adjusted (discounted) rate of return at least equal to the estimated cost of capital. Present estimates are that the cost of capital is 15% after tax.
3. Accepted proposals should average over their lifetime an adjusted rate of return on assets employed (calculated in the conventional accounting method) at least equal to the average rate of return on total assets shown by the statutory financial statements.

Present a report, showing all relevant calculations, which will indicate to the management whether or not the proposal to purchase this milling machine meets each of the selection criteria.

Solution
We can calculate the profit and cash flow figures as follows:

Z Co. Ltd

	Year				
	1	2	3	4	5
Sales	6600	7200	7800	8000	8000
Operating costs	3200	3200	3200	3200	3200
	3400	4000	4600	4800	4800
Depreciation/tax	2200	2200	2200	2200	2200
Allowance					
	1200	1800	2400	2600	2600
Taxation	600	900	1200	1300	1300
Profit after tax	600	900	1200	1300	1300
Cash flow	2800	3100	3400	3500	3500

Note that the depreciation/tax allowance figure is *not* a cash expense and must be added back to the profit figure to get the annual cash flow. Another point to note is that in this example, accounting depreciation and tax allowances are the same. This will rarely be the case in practice and separate tax computations are usually required of the charge for taxation. There may also be timing differences with tax payments as they may be paid in a later year to that to which they actually relate.

We can see that the payback period is less than four years, thus satisfying one of the screening criteria. However, DCF methods give alternative advice; using discount rate of 15%,

$$
\begin{aligned}
\text{NPV} &= -11\,000 + 2800\,(0.8696) \\
&\quad + 3100\,(0.7561) + 3400\,(0.6575) \\
&\quad + 3500\,(0.5718) + 3500\,(0.4972) \\
&= -244 \\
\text{IRR} &= 14.1\%
\end{aligned}
$$

Both NPV and IRR reject the project.
Accounting rate of return:

$$
\begin{aligned}
\text{Average profit} &= (600 + 900 + 1200 + 1300 + 1300)/5 \\
&= 1060 \\[4pt]
\text{Average capital employed} &= \frac{11\,000}{2} \\
&= 5500 \\[4pt]
\text{ARR} &= \frac{1060}{5500} \times 100 \\
&= 19.3\%
\end{aligned}
$$

The project meets two of the three tests, payback and accounting rate of return both favouring the project. However, when discounting methods are used the project is rejected. There is a negative NPV when a discount rate of 15% is used and the project has an IRR below the required rate of return. The project should therefore be rejected.

This example illustrates how it is possible for alternative methods of project appraisal to give conflicting advice. In this case, use of the non-discounting methods, payback and accounting return, would have led to the adoption of a project which failed to meet the cost of financing.

Choosing between projects (mutually exclusive projects)

Now let us consider what happens if we have to choose between alternative projects. We have already seen that Payback and ARR are unreliable even for the simplest of accept/reject decisions and they are equally unreliable for choosing between mutually exclusive projects. Can NPV and IRR both be relied on to give the same correct advice? Unfortunately not. Consider the following example:

| | Year | | | | | NPV at | |
	0	1	2	3	4	15%	IRR
Project A	−50 000	+10 000	+25 000	+25 000	+25 000	8 331	22%
Project B	−10 000	+5 000	+5 000	+5 000	+1 000	1 988	26%

We can thus see that while NPV favours project A, project B has the highest IRR. In these circumstances NPV will give the correct advice indicating that A is preferable to B because it makes us better off. The reasons that IRR can give alternative advice in these and other situations is that

1. IRR is a rate of return while NPV is a measure of wealth. Therefore the scale of investment is important.
2. All DCF methods assume that deficit cash balances are charged interest at the rate of discount and earn interest on positive cash balances at this rate. This is known as the 'reinvestment principle'. Thus the pattern of cash flows over time can affect the size of the IRR.
3. There are also technical problems with the use of IRR: where cash flows are non-conventional, in that rather than having an initial cash outflow followed by a stream of cash receipts there are further cash outflows later in the life of the project, there can be more than one IRR solution.

If it is wished to use IRR in choosing between pairs of projects then it is necessary to calculate the IRR on the extra or incremental investment in the larger project. If this IRR is greater than the company cost of capital it will indicate that the extra investment is justified.

The incremental investment in the previous example is as follows:

			Year			NPV at	
	0	1	2	3	4	15%	IRR
Project A	−50 000	+10 000	+25 000	+25 000	+25 000	8 331	22%
Project B	−10 000	+5 000	+5 000	+5 000	+1 000	1 988	26%
Project A − B	−40 000	+5 000	+20 000	+20 000	+24 000	6 343	21%

This shows that the extra investment is worthwhile and supports the NPV decision. In fact we are seeing that NPV's advice is more reliable than IRR's and this is usually the case. The example also illustrates how NPVs can be added together. The NPV of project A is equal to the sum of the NPVs of B and A − B.

Advantages and disadvantages of appraisal methods

We can summarize the four techniques of project appraisal examined as follows:

NPV

1. Measures the immediate increase in wealth which results from the adoption of a project when discounted at the company cost of capital.
2. Gives most reliable advice for accept/reject decisions and mutually exclusive decisions.
3. Allows for the time value of money.
4. NPVs are additive. That is the total benefit of a number of projects can be obtained by summing the individual NPVs to give a total value for wealth increase.
5. NPV is sometimes criticized on the basis that non-financial managers

find it difficult to comprehend and find rates of return (IRR and ARR) and payback easier to relate to.

IRR

1. Gives a rate of interest over the life of the project which can be compared with the company's cost of capital.
2. In most accept/reject decisions advice given by IRR will coincide with that given by NPV. However, IRR has technical problems where there are unconventional cash flows (multiple IRRs) and may give incorrect advice where a choice has to be made between mutually exclusive projects.
3. IRR is often favoured over NPV in practice because, as mentioned above, businessmen find it easier to relate to. However, IRR must not be confused with ARR which is an entirely different and less reliable measure.

Payback

1. Measures how long (usually how many years) the project takes to pay back in cash the initial investment.
2. This method is often favoured by businessmen because it is claimed that it emphasizes liquidity and makes an intuitive allowance for risk. It is also simple to use and easy to understand.
3. However, use of payback alone can lead to the selection of unprofitable projects and while it could be argued that its use as a secondary screening process could be useful, in some circumstances it has many drawbacks.
4. No recognition is given to the time value of money. Cash flows receivable after the payback period are ignored.
5. Risk is related to the speed of payback which may not be realistic.
6. The use of payback will tend to favour short-term projects which may lead to the adoption of unprofitable or low profit short-term projects and the exclusion of long-term profitable projects. This could be particularly crucial where the introduction of new technology is being considered.

ARR

1. Gives a measure of average accounting rate of return over the life of the project. The previous three methods all use cash flows. This is the only method using accounting profit.
2. Measurement of accounting profit and capital employed can both contain areas of subjectivity (e.g. depreciation, research and development, valuation of assets).
3. ARR does not consider the time value of money; a major flaw.
4. However, company managers are well acquainted with the measure and indeed are often appraised on the basis of profits (EPS) and profitability (rate of return on assets). In these circumstances, perhaps it is unsurprising that managers are concerned about the effect of a project on accounting profits and profitability, but unless the project

is large relative to the company it would be surprising if it had a significant effect on overall accounting profitability.

Conclusions

NPV is the most reliable method of project appraisal and is in accord with the principle of maximizing shareholders' wealth. However, in practice other methods are also used. IRR, because it also takes into consideration the time value of money and managers find it easier to use; payback, because it stresses liquidity and seems to allow for risk; ARR, because managers are appraised using this measure and consider it of importance. However, managers wishing to maximize the welfare of investors should use NPV while perhaps also computing IRR, payback and ARR as inputs to the decision-making process.

4 Further problems in project appraisal

Introduction

In this chapter we consider further problems which the project appraiser may encounter and further factors which have to be considered in carrying out appraisals. We begin by considering what happens to the NPV decision rule for choosing between alternative projects if projects themselves are capable of replication. This insight enables us to calculate optimum replacement times for machines which need replacing from time to time.

The effect of inflation on project appraisal is then discussed. This is an important topic given the high levels of inflation experienced in the UK and other countries in recent years. Failure to incorporate allowance for inflation properly in our project appraisal could lead to good projects being rejected or poor projects being undertaken. There could also be a tendency for short-term projects to be favoured over more profitable long-term projects.

We conclude with a brief look at capital rationing. In this instance it is emphasized that, as with any other factor in short supply, it is a case of maximizing, in this case NPV, per unit of scarce resource.

Appraising repeatable projects

In the previous chapter, when projects were compared the implicit assumption was made that they could only be undertaken once. We were concerned only with identifying the best single project in terms of size of NPV irrespective of the life-span of competing projects. However, we must recognize that there may be situations where projects may be repeatable and that to compare the NPVs of projects with different lives may not be correct.

Let us suppose we have two mutually exclusive projects with cash flows as follows:

	t_0	t_1	t_2	t_3	t_4	NPV at 10%
A	$-10\,000$	$+4\,000$	$+4\,000$	$+4\,000$	$+4\,000$	$+2\,679$
B	$-8\,000$	$+6\,000$	$+6\,000$	—	—	$+2\,413$

Project A lasts for four years, B only for two. On the basis of NPV alone A appears better, but what if project B could be repeated? In this case we could compare A with the two project Bs as follows:

	t_0	t_1	t_2	t_3	t_4	NPV at 10%
A	−10 000	+4 000	+4 000	+4 000	+4 000	+2 679
B1	−8 000	+6 000	+6 000			
B2			−8 000	+6 000	+6 000	
B1 + 2	−8 000	+6 000	−2 000	+6 000	+6 000	+4 408

Or NPV of two Project Bs = 2413 + 2413 (0.8264)
$$= +4407 \text{ (difference in rounding)}$$

We can now see that when the ability to repeat project B is taken into account that B is the superior investment. In this case it was comparatively easy to compare A with B by replicating B for another time cycle. However, if we were comparing, say, a seven year project with an 11 year project it would be necessary to consider a time scale of 77 years! We can instead compute the annual equivalent annuity of NPVs by multiplying each NPV by the annual equivalent annuity (AE) factor appropriate to the life in years and discount rate used. The AE factors (see Table 1.3) show the annual amount equivalent to £1 of NPV for varying interest rates and numbers of years. AE factors are the reciprocals of annuity factors (Table 1.2).

If we take the original single project NPVs calculated, then the annual equivalent annuities are

$$A = 2679 \times 0.3155 = £845.22$$
$$B = 2413 \times 0.5762 = £1390.37$$

We can see that B has the greater annual value and is therefore the preferred project. If it was intended to repeat the projects indefinitely, then a perpetuity value could be calculated by dividing the annual equivalent annuity by the discount rate used.

$$\text{Perpetuity value for B} = \frac{1390.37}{0.1}$$
$$= £13\,903.7$$

Optimum replacement cycle

In the illustrations above, whole projects incorporating costs and benefits have been used. However, the technique can also be used with costs alone to determine the optimum replacement time for pieces of plant. For example, suppose we regularly replace motor cars within four years and wish to determine the optimum replacement cycle; the costs and trade-in value of the car are estimated as follows:

Table 1.3 Annual Equivalent Annuity $\dfrac{r}{1-(1+r)^{-n}}$

Years (n)	Interest rates (r)										
	6	7	8	9	10	11	12	13	14	15	
1	1.0600	1.0700	1.0800	1.0900	1.1000	1.1100	1.1200	1.1300	1.1400	1.1500	1
2	0.5454	0.5531	0.5608	0.5685	0.5762	0.5839	0.5917	0.5995	0.6073	0.6151	2
3	0.3741	0.3811	0.3880	0.3951	0.4021	0.4092	0.4163	0.4235	0.4307	0.4380	3
4	0.2886	0.2952	0.3019	0.3087	0.3155	0.3223	0.3292	0.3362	0.3432	0.3503	4
5	0.2374	0.2439	0.2505	0.2571	0.2638	0.2706	0.2774	0.2843	0.2913	0.2983	5
6	0.2034	0.2098	0.2163	0.2229	0.2296	0.2364	0.2432	0.2502	0.2572	0.2642	6
7	0.1791	0.1856	0.1921	0.1987	0.2054	0.2122	0.2191	0.2261	0.2332	0.2404	7
8	0.1610	0.1675	0.1740	0.1807	0.1874	0.1943	0.2013	0.2084	0.2156	0.2229	8
9	0.1470	0.1535	0.1601	0.1668	0.1736	0.1806	0.1877	0.1949	0.2022	0.2096	9
10	0.1359	0.1424	0.1490	0.1558	0.1627	0.1698	0.1770	0.1843	0.1917	0.1993	10
11	0.1268	0.1334	0.1401	0.1469	0.1540	0.1611	0.1684	0.1758	0.1834	0.1911	11
12	0.1193	0.1259	0.1327	0.1397	0.1468	0.1540	0.1614	0.1690	0.1767	0.1845	12
13	0.1130	0.1197	0.1265	0.1336	0.1408	0.1482	0.1557	0.1634	0.1712	0.1791	13
14	0.1076	0.1143	0.1213	0.1284	0.1357	0.1432	0.1509	0.1587	0.1666	0.1747	14
15	0.1030	0.1098	0.1168	0.1241	0.1315	0.1391	0.1468	0.1547	0.1628	0.1710	15

	t_0	t_1	t_2	t_3	t_4		
Cost of new car	12 000						
Running costs		1 000	1 500	1 500	2 000		
Trade-in value at end of year		9 000	7 000	5 000	2 500		
Cash flows of operating car for years						*NPV at 10%*	*AE value*
1	12 000	−8 000				4 727	5 200
2	12 000	1 000	−5 500			8 364	4 819
3	12 000	1 000	1 500	−3 500		11 519	4 632
4	12 000	1 000	1 500	1 500	−500	14 934	4 712

The best policy would be to replace the car every three years as this gives the lowest annual cost. The technique is a neat way to compare projects with different life spans and to obtain optimum replacement advice. However, we must recognize that the computations we have carried out assume that benefits and costs remain constant over time and that this applies both to initial capital costs and annual costs and benefits.

Inflation in project appraisal

Inflation, the change in price levels, must be considered when undertaking project analysis. This should be self evident when we are considering activities covering a number of years; however, it is not always taken into account, or if it is, it is sometimes treated incorrectly. **Expected inflation** is usually assumed to be reflected in current interest rates; if higher inflation is expected then money market interest rates would be expected to be higher. **Real** interest rates are rates after stripping out expected inflation. The relationship between interest rates and inflation can be summarized by the equation

$$(1 + m) = (1 + r)(1 + i)$$

Where m is the money or market rate of interest, r is the real rate of interest and i the anticipated level of inflation. As the money market rate is usually used in appraising projects, to be consistent all projected cash flows should reflect anticipated inflation; an alternative would be for all cash flows to be stated in current terms and for a real interest rate to be used in the analysis. As money and real rates can vary by 10% or more it is vital to ensure that inflation is treated consistently and correctly in project appraisal.

Suppose that estimates have been made for a project in current terms as follows:

t_0	t_1	t_2	t_3
−6000	+3000	+2000	+2000

If the cash flows are discounted at the market rate of interest of 15% there is a negative NPV of −£564 and the IRR is 8.8%. However, all cash flows are stated in today's money and future years should be adjusted for inflation or a real rate of interest used for discounting. If the real interest rate was 5% the NPV would be £399 positive while the IRR would of course still be 8.8%.

It can be shown that given constant inflation and interest rates the same result can be obtained either by discounting values stated in current terms at the real rate or discounting inflation adjusted forecasts at the market rate.

For example, in the illustration above the market rate was said to be 15% and the real rate 5%; this implies an inflation rate of $9\frac{1}{2}\%$ calculated as follows:

$$(1 + m) = (1 + r)(1 + i)$$
$$i = \frac{1 + m}{1 + r} - 1$$
$$= \frac{1 + 0.15}{1 + 0.05} - 1$$
$$= \underline{0.095 \ (9\tfrac{1}{2}\%)}$$

If instead of discounting the cash flows at 5% we had increased years 1 to 3 by $9\frac{1}{2}\%$ compound and then discounted at 15% we would have obtained the same result. Doing this we get

$$NPV = -6000 + \frac{3000(1.095)}{(1.15)} + \frac{2000(1.095)^2}{(1.15)^2}$$
$$+ \frac{2000(1.095)^3}{(1.15)}$$
$$= \underline{+396} \text{ (difference due to rounding inflation figure)}$$

It is therefore very important either to allow for inflation in making cash flow forecasts and to discount at the market rate of interest, or to state cash flows in today's (current) values and discount at the real rate of interest. We can see with the example that if market rates are used to discount forecasts stated in current values worthwhile projects might be rejected. Because not all costs and benefits are affected in precisely the same way by inflation it will usually be best to allow explicitly for anticipated price rises in each factor separately before calculating the net cash flow for each year.

Capital rationing

In our discussion to date it has been assumed that there are sufficient financial resources to undertake all projects considered as desirable which would normally mean all those projects having positive NPVs. However, we need to consider how our decision rule would be modified if there was some constraint on the amount of investment funds available. This state of affairs is normally referred to as capital rationing.

Capital rationing, the lack of funds to undertake positive NPV projects, should not occur, at least not in the medium to long term, in well functioning capital markets. However, sometimes companies themselves limit the amount of new investment resources and for this reason capital rationing is often split between soft capital rationing and hard capital rationing. Soft capital rationing refers to those situations where the company itself limits the amount of investment funds in any particular period. This may be imposed by management perhaps because it is felt that growth should be limited to current management capabilities. Hard capital rationing arises when the constraint is externally imposed. As previously stated, in perfectly functioning capital markets this situation should not occur, but it is possible that banks might impose borrowing limits, particularly in the case of smaller businesses.

If capital is constrained then it is necessary to maximize the contribution per unit of scarce resource, just as would be the case with any other scarce resource.

In the simplest capital rationing situation, funds are assumed to be constrained for a single period only and in addition it is assumed that all projects may be undertaken in whole or in part.

Example
Suppose a company is faced with the following six projects but that capital is restricted to £90 000 for the current period.

			Year			NPV at	
Project	t_0	t_1	t_2	t_3	t_4	10%	IRR
A	−30 000	5 000	10 000	13 000	15 000	2 822	13.6
B	−20 000	13 000	13 000	—	—	2 562	19.4
C	−50 000	10 000	10 000	25 000	25 000	3 214	12.5
D	−10 000	4 000	4 000	4 000	4 000	2 679	21.9
E	−20 000	23 000	—	—	—	909	15.0
F	−40 000	15 000	20 000	10 000	10 000	4 509	15.6

If we selected projects on the basis of highest NPV then the choice would be

Project	NPV	INV
F	4 509	40 000
C	3 214	50 000
	£7 723	£90 000

If selection was on the basis of highest IRRs then the choice would be

Project	NPV	INV
D	2 679	10 000
B	2 562	20 000
F	4 509	40 000
E	909	20 000
	£10 659	£90 000

Although ranking by IRR in this case produces a higher NPV than ranking by size of NPV, neither of these would give the optimal selection; instead the projects must be ranked on the ratio of NPV to investment outlay.

This ratio is called the benefit–cost ratio and using this criteria the projects selected would be

Project	NPV	INV	NPV/INV
D	2 679	10 000	0.27
B	2 562	20 000	0.13
F	4 509	40 000	0.11
A($\frac{2}{3}$)	1 881	20 000	0.09
	£11 631	£90 000	

Projects C and E with benefit–cost ratios of 0.06 and 0.05 respectively would be eliminated.

We can see that this gives a superior total NPV. A similar ranking and result would be given by using the ratio of gross present value to investment outlay. This ratio is called the profitability index (P/I).

The technique used above assumes single-period capital rationing and that projects are divisible. If projects are not divisible the problem becomes one of integer programming. However, an approximate method could be used by adopting projects in ranking order until the point where the next project is adopted in full would go beyond the funds available. At this point the decision maker should review the projects still available and adopt those with highest NPV within budget of funds still available. In the example above we would adopt projects D, B and F. As projects are assumed not to be divisible, A could not be adopted and project E would have to be undertaken as this is the only available project which could be undertaken within the capital constraint.

If capital is rationed in more than one period (multi-period capital rationing) then linear programming (LP) will have to be used to formulate and obtain the optimum mix of projects. Use of LP will assume that the projects are divisible; if they are not, then integer programming will have to be used.

5 Introduction to risk in project appraisal

Introduction

Having examined techniques of project appraisal and concluded that DCF methods provide the most accurate advice to decision makers, with NPV being more reliable than IRR, we need to examine how risk and uncertainty impact on project appraisal and the decision maker.

A theoretical distinction is sometimes made between risk and uncertainty. However, in practical decision making the two terms tend to be used interchangeably. We shall do this, relating risk and uncertainty to situations where decision makers are unsure about the outcome of future cash flows. There will be very few business decisions where risk is absent; taking risks is the essence of entrepreneural activity.

Approaches to risk appraisal

We can identify two distinct but related approaches to analysing risk in project appraisal.

1. The analysis of project risk in a unified investment framework enabling projects to be ranked in terms of their risk and required return so that analysts may identify risk-adjusted rates of return specific to individual projects.
2. Project analysis where techniques of numerical analysis are used to analyse individual projects to identify factors making that particular project risky.

The first approach is based on the simple idea that investors in projects will require higher returns from riskier projects. The problems are: how is risk to be defined? And how much extra return should be demanded per unit of risk?

Risk premia

Initially risk premia (extra return) were determined within individual companies on an arbitrary basis. For example, investment for cost saving might have been required to show a lower return than investment for expanding current activities, which itself might be expected to show a lower return than investment in a new type of business activity. The problem with this type of approach is that it depends on the manager's perception of risk and is not based on any rational and sustainable view of risk. Fortunately in more recent years a theory has become available which enables a much more rational approach to be taken to the calculation of risk premia. The rest of this chapter is concerned with examining the background to this approach, while discussion of the techniques of project analysis is deferred until Chapter 7.

Shareholder and project risk

We begin our formal examination of risk in project appraisal by considering who it is that carries the ultimate risk of failure when projects are undertaken. We should be able to see that it is the investors providing funds for the project who lose out if things go wrong, and ultimately the equity or ordinary shareholders of companies who bear this loss. On the other hand if the project is highly successful then it is these same investors who will reap the rewards.

The fact that it is company managers who make decisions on whether to invest or not should not conceal the fact that it is the investor whose money is at risk. The company can be viewed as a convenient administrative device enabling funds to be collected from many different investors for investment in real projects. Figure 5.1 illustrates this point. This diagram helps to make another important point. Project risk and shareholder risk are one and the same. The returns to shareholders are dependent upon the returns earned on projects. It can perhaps be better appreciated if we consider a situation where we have a single shareholder investing in a company undertaking one project. There would surely be no argument that shareholder and project risk coincided. The introduction of more shareholders and more projects will not alter the principle but only make the analysis a little more difficult.

It should be apparent that if managers want to know how risky projects are and what return should be demanded from particular projects then they should be asking how equity investors view risk and determine return.

This is the basis of the current most popular approach to analysing and determining risk and return. The theory is embodied in the Capital Asset Pricing Model (CAPM) which has its roots in portfolio theory, originally

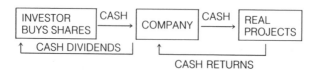

Fig. 5.1. Flow of financial and real investment funds.

developed by Harry Markowitz in the context of investment in the ordinary shares of companies.

Portfolio theory

Portfolio theory is based on the assumption that investors appraise their investments on the basis of

1. Expected return ($\bar{E}$);
2. Variance, or more usually Standard Deviation (SD), of expected returns.

When making a single investment if two shares had the same return then the one with lower SD would be preferred or if both had the same SD then the one with highest $\bar{E}$ would be preferred. However, the important point stressed by Markowitz was that when shares were held together (i.e. in portfolios) that more efficient investment resulted because the returns on individual securities tended to be less than perfectly correlated. That is, if in a particular situation one company did poorly there was a good chance that this would be compensated by another company doing better. This idea can be illustrated in the context of the smallest portfolio possible, a two security portfolio.

	Security	
	A	B
Expected returns ($\bar{E}$)	10%	12%
Standard deviation (SD)	12%	20%

Let us suppose we invest 50% (0.5) of our wealth in each security. Then the expected return of our portfolio,

$$\bar{E}_p = (0.5 \times 0.10) + (0.5 \times 0.12)$$
$$= \underline{0.11\ (11\%)}$$

Thus the expected portfolio return is simply the value weighted average of the expected returns of the individual security. In general we could write

$$\bar{E}_p = \Sigma\, W_i E_i$$

Where W_i represents the proportion of wealth invested in security i. However the standard deviation of our portfolio is a little more complex,

$$SD = \sqrt{(0.5^2 \times 0.12^2) + (0.5^2 \times 0.20^2) + 2(0.5 \times 0.5)\,Cov_{AB}}$$

We cannot sum standard deviations, so instead work with variances then take the square root to get standard deviation. The first two items on the right-hand side we can see are the proportions invested in each security and the standard deviations, squared in both cases as we are working with variances. The third and final item introduces another term, Cov_{AB}. This is the covariance of the returns of A with those of B and is a measure of the extent to which the returns of each vary one with another in different conditions. The covariance is multiplied by the proportion invested in each security and by two as it is necessary to consider the covariance of A with B and B with A; these are of course the same.

The covariance term can also be expressed in terms of each securities' standard deviation and the correlation coefficient of returns between that pair of securities. Thus,

$$\text{Cov}_{AB} = K_{AB} S_{DA} SD_B$$

where K_{AB} is the correlation coefficient.

The correlation coefficient can take on values between $+1$ (perfect positive correlation) and -1 (perfect negative correlation).

With

$K_{AB} = 1$
$SD_p = \sqrt{(0.5^2 \times 0.12^2) + (0.5^2 \times 0.20^2) + 2(0.5 \times 0.5 \times (+1) \times 0.12 \times 0.20)}$
    $= 0.16 \ (16\%)$

With

$K_{AB} = -1$
$SD_p = \sqrt{(0.5^2 \times 0.12^2) + (0.5^2 \times 0.20^2) + 2(0.5 \times 0.5 \times (-1) \times 0.12 \times 0.20)}$
    $= 0.04 \ (4\%)$

With perfect positive correlation the standard deviation is merely a value weighted average of the standard deviations of the two securities, however with perfect negative correlation there is substantial reduction in risk. In fact with perfect negative correlation it would be possible to construct a fully hedged portfolio with zero standard deviation.

In general the standard deviation of a two-security portfolio can be written as

$$SD_p = \sqrt{W_A^2 SD_A^2 + W_B^2 SD_B^2 + 2W_A W_B K_{AB} SD_A SD_B}$$

Although correlation limits lie between $+1$ and -1, in practice it is found that most securities have positive correlations of less than $+1$. However,

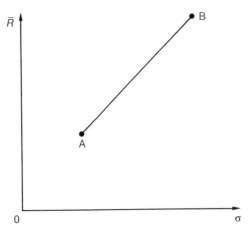

Fig. 5.2. Perfect positive correlation.

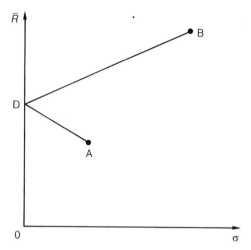

Fig. 5.3. Perfect negative correlation. At *D* a perfectly hedged portfolio with zero risk is obtained.

provided correlation is less than perfect, more efficient combinations of securities can be obtained by combining more and more securities together. 'Efficient' in this context means that the portfolios obtained give a higher return for their level of risk as measured by standard deviation or a lower risk for their level of return.

The portfolio discussion can be represented in diagrammatic form (Figs 5.2–5.5).

As more securities are added to a portfolio, so the scope for risk reduction and the creation of more efficient portfolios increases. This gives rise to the identification of an efficient set of portfolios which will dominate all other portfolios. These efficient portfolios will give the highest return

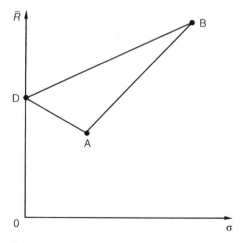

Fig. 5.4. Limits of diversification. All possible portfolios lie within *ADB*.

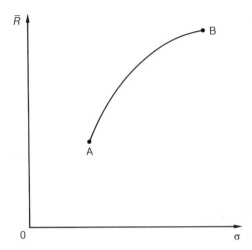

Fig. 5.5.   Correlation of +0.5.

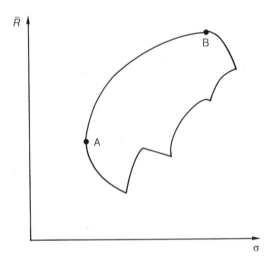

Fig. 5.6.   All possible portfolios with AB the efficient set.

for that level of risk or have the lowest risk for that level of return. This is illustrated in Fig. 5.6.

Capital market line

All investors will want to invest in an efficient portfolio but the particular portfolio each individual chooses will depend upon their attitude to risk and return. However, if we now consider another possibility that investors can lend and borrow at a risk-free rate of interest we find that the choice

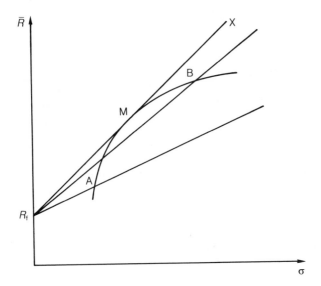

Fig. 5.7.   Efficient portfolios and risk-free lending and borrowing.

of risky portfolio is the same for all investors. Figure 5.7 illustrates this point. With the introduction of risk-free borrowing and lending the efficient set of portfolios changes from the curve AMB to the straight line R_fMX. All investors will want to invest in a combination of risk-free lending and borrowing, together with the portfolio of risky securities located at M. This portfolio at M will be the market portfolio, being composed of all the available securities in the market.

If R_f is the risk-free rate of interest, $\bar{R}_m$ the expected market return and SD_f, SD_m the respective standard deviations we can write the expected return and standard deviation of these (two security) portfolios as follows:

$$\bar{E}_p = W_f R_f + W_m \bar{R}_m$$
$$SD_p = \sqrt{W_f^2 SD_f^2 + W_m^2 SD_m^2 + 2W_f W_m K_{fm} SD_f SD_m}$$

But $SD_f = 0 = K_{fm}$

$$\therefore SD_p = W_m SD_m \text{ or } W_m = \frac{SD_p}{SD_m}$$

As all our wealth is invested in the two security portfolio,

$$W_f + W_m = 1$$
$$W_f = 1 - W_m$$

We may write

$$\bar{E}_p = (1 - W_m) R_f + W_m \bar{R}_m$$
$$\bar{E}_p = R_f + W_m(\bar{R}_m - R_f)$$

Substituting $W_m = \frac{SD_p}{SD_m}$

$$\overline{E}_p = R_f + \frac{(\overline{R}_m - R_f)\,SD_p}{SD_m}$$

This is the equation for the portfolios lying on the capital market line. It says that the expected return of such portfolios is composed of the risk-free rate of return plus a risk premium which is dependent upon the standard deviation of the portfolio. This equation only applies to portfolios composed of an investment in the risk-free asset and the market portfolio of risky assets.

If we assume that it is possible to invest funds in this way then all investors will do so. It is assumed that investors are rational and will seek to maximize returns per unit of risk and by following this strategy they will be able to do this. If investors do invest in this way, what are the implications?

Capital asset pricing model

Figure 5.8 shows how risk is reduced as securities are added to a portfolio. Initially there is substantial risk reduction with comparatively modest numbers of securities. However, there are diminishing gains as numbers increase and no matter how large the portfolio some risk remains. Portfolio diversification allows unique risk relating to individual securities to be eliminated but market risk remains. Market risk affects all securities to a greater or lesser degree and its effect can be particularly observed in times of substantial market movement. Therefore if investors hold the market portfolio they will still face risk but only market risk, all unique risk having been diversified away. If unique risk can be eliminated then the market will price securities on the basis of their market risk alone. This reasoning is the basis of the Capital Asset Pricing Model (CAPM). CAPM assumes the following:

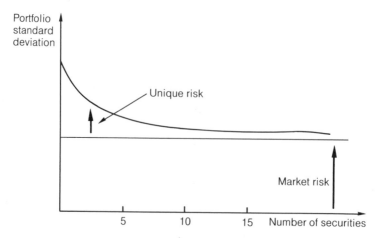

Fig. 5.8. Unique risk eliminated but market risk remains.

1. Risk averse investors who appraise securities on the basis of expected return and standard deviation or variance of return.
2. All investors have the same single-period planning horizon.
3. Homogenous expectations; all market participants have the same views on future returns and risk.
4. Perfect market exists with no taxes or transaction costs.
5. It is possible to borrow and lend freely at the riskless rate of interest.

In such a market all investors investing in risky securities will be holding the market portfolio.

It can be shown that the rate of return on any individual asset, $\bar{R}_i$ can be written as

$$\bar{R}_i = R_f + \beta_i (\bar{R}_m - R_f)$$

Expected return = Risk free return + Risk premium

R_f is the risk-free rate of return and $\bar{R}_m$ the expected return on the market portfolio. The beta (β) factor which determines the size of the risk premium is a function of the correlation between the asset returns and the market. By definition the market has a beta of one.

Securities with betas greater than one will rise and fall more rapidly than the market and are termed aggressive securities while securities with below average betas, less than one, are called defensive securities as they will fall less quickly and rise more slowly than the market.

The beta can be decomposed as follows:

$$\beta_i = \frac{Cov_{im}}{SD_m^2}$$
$$= \frac{K_{im} SD_i SD_m}{SD_m^2}$$
$$= \frac{K_{im} SD_i}{SD_m}$$

We can see that beta depends on the degree of correlation between security returns and the market. It is quite possible for securities with high total risk as measured by standard deviation to have less than average betas.

Example
A security i has a standard deviation of returns of 40% and a correlation coefficient of returns with the market of 0.5. If the expected return on the market is 18% with standard deviation of 25% and the risk-free rate is 9%, what is the beta and expected return of i?

Solution

$$\beta_i = \frac{0.5 \times 0.4}{0.25}$$
$$= 0.8$$
$$\bar{R}_i = 0.09 + 0.8 (0.18 - 0.09)$$
$$= 0.162 \ (16.2\%)$$

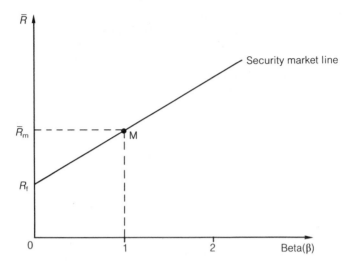

Fig. 5.9.   Security market line.

i has a higher standard deviation than the market but a below average beta and required return because of its low correlation with the market. CAPM can be represented by the Security Market Line (SML) as illustrated in Fig. 5.9.

In equilibrium all securities will plot along the SML. Portfolio risk as measured by beta is easy to calculate as it is the sum of the value-weighted average of the individual securities in the portfolio.

$$\beta_p = \Sigma \ W_i B_i$$

If investors hold diversified portfolios, then beta rather than total risk, as measured by standard deviation, is the appropriate measure of security risk. It follows that assets in general will be priced according to their market risk and in the following chapter we apply this theory to the measurement of risk in project appraisal.

6 Capital asset pricing model and project appraisal

Introduction

We saw in the previous chapter how risk could be reduced by holding a portfolio of securities. Ultimately by holding the market portfolio an investor could diversify away all unique or non-market risk and be left facing only market risk. In such a situation the measure of risk would no longer be total risk, as measured by standard deviation, but market risk, as measured by beta. In this chapter we develop these ideas into a practical means of assessing project returns. This approach is summarized as follows:

1. Managers appraising projects should relate return required to that required by investors in companies of equivalent risk.
2. Investors are assumed to be rational and hold portfolios which diversify away all non-market risk.
3. As non-market risk can be eliminated the market will price risk on the basis of systematic or market risk only.
4. The measure of risk will be beta (β) which measures the covariance of returns with the market as a whole.

The expected return $\bar{R}_i$, on any project under appraisal could be written as

$$\bar{R}_i = R_f + B_i(\bar{R}_m - R_f)$$

Adapting the model for practical use

To make use of this *ex ante* model we need values for

R_f = Current short term risk-free interest rate
B_i = Beta of project
$\bar{R}_m$ = Expected market return for next period

or

$(\bar{R}_m - R_f)$ = Expected market risk premium for next period

Two adaptations are usually made when using the model in practice. Firstly the model is used for multi-period projects and secondly historic data are used to compute relevant betas and market risk premia.

The short-term risk-free rate most appropriate to the model is the rate currently being earned on government three month treasury bills. However, with a longer-term project a more appropriate rate might be the yield to maturity of a government security having the same life as that expected on the project.

Risk information, including betas, are available for most quoted companies. The London Business School (LBS) publishes a quarterly Risk Measurement Service containing betas and other information relating not only to individual companies but to industries as well. The use of commercial services in obtaining project betas is discussed in detail below.

The final need is to estimate either the expected market return or the expected market risk premium over the life of the project. Once again historic data are used because of the difficulty of estimating expectations. Research shows that in the UK over a 60 year period the risk premium $(\overline{R}_m - R_f)$ has averaged around 9% per annum. Use of this long-run average assumes that actual returns reflect expectations and that historic premia are a guide to future premia.

Use of commercial beta services

We now consider in more detail the use of betas obtained from commercial services and will relate our discussion to the LBS Risk Measurement

Table 6.1 London Business School, Risk Measurement Service, industry betas

Bricks and roofing tiles	1.10
Contracting and construction	1.03
Miscellaneous mechanical engineering	1.11
Machine and other tools	0.93
Electronics	1.02
Radio and television	1.10
Motor components	1.19
Breweries	0.83
Leisure	0.95
General food manufacturing	0.88
Food retailing	0.83
Clothing	0.92
Tobacco	1.14
Oil	0.89
Banks	0.95
Property	0.97
Rubbers	0.77
Teas	0.56
Gold	0.80

Service mentioned earlier. This service lists betas of ordinary shares for quoted companies including those quoted on the USM and Third Market. The betas are computed using a standard least square regression program based on the monthly returns of each security over the previous five years and the market return as represented by FT actuaries all share index over the same period.

In the case of an all equity company where a project under appraisal was of the same average risk as those currently being undertaken by the company then the beta of the equity would be an appropriate measure of risk. However, if the company was contemplating a different type of activity then a beta appropriate to that activity should be used. This could be the average beta of a group of companies carrying out a similar activity or an industry beta could be used from the LBS tables. Table 6.1 shows industry betas taken from these tables.

The general level of betas is what we might expect with higher betas being associated with those activities having a higher correlation with mainstream economic activities. Note that gold, although having high total risk, as measured by standard deviation, has a lower than average beta, because historically it has been a counter-cyclical investment attracting more interest when investors are disenchanted with general stock-market investment.

Ungearing betas

Whether we use individual equity betas or industry betas, we need to be aware that as well as reflecting the risk of the underlying business activities, these betas will also reflect financial risk brought about by the existence of debt in the capital structure of the company(ies).

Before geared equity betas can be used in project appraisal they must be 'ungeared'.

If B_A, B_E and B_D represent asset beta, equity beta and debt beta respectively, then assuming a taxless world,

$$B_A = B_E \frac{E}{E + D} + B_D \frac{D}{E + D}$$

With E and D representing the market value of equity and debt. If debt can be regarded as risk-free the second term on the right-hand side of the equation drops out (i.e. $B_D = 0$) and we have

$$B_A = B_E \frac{E}{E + D}$$

With company taxation debt interest becomes tax deductible and we have

$$B_A = B_E \frac{E}{E + D(1 - t)}$$

$$B_A = B_E \frac{1}{1 + \frac{D}{E}(1 - t)}$$

A similar adjustment would have to be made to any industry beta used, if not already adjusted, to reflect the average level of gearing in the industry.

Example

Hem Motors is a family owned unquoted company in the motor industry. It has a current debt to equity ratio of 0.30. The average equity beta for a group of similar companies in the motor industry is 1.3; their average debt to equity ratio is 0.20. The risk-free rate of return is currently 12%, the market risk premium is assumed to be 9% and the effective tax is estimated to be 30%.

1. What is the required return on the assets of Hem Motors?
2. What is the required return on the equity of Hem Motors?

The ungeared equity beta for the industry will enable us to calculate a required return for Hem's assets.

$$B_A = B_E \frac{1}{1 + \dfrac{D}{E}(1 - t)}$$

$$= 1.3 \frac{1}{1 + (0.2)(1 - 0.3)}$$

$$= 1.3 \frac{1}{1.14}$$

$$= \underline{1.14}$$

$$R_A = \underline{0.12 + 1.14\,(9)}$$
$$= \underline{0.2226\,(22.26\%)}$$

We can obtain the required return on Hem's equity by using the asset beta geared up to reflect Hem's level of gearing:

$$B_E = B_A\left(1 + \frac{D}{E}(1 - t)\right)$$

$$B_E = 1.14(1 + 0.3 \times 0.7)$$
$$= \underline{1.38}$$

$$R_E = \underline{0.12 + 1.38\,(9)}$$
$$= \underline{0.2442\,(24.42\%)}$$

The example showed how even an unquoted company can obtain information on project required returns by using average industry betas of quoted companies. Use of historic betas assumes that betas are stable over time. Evidence suggests that portfolio betas are more reliable in this respect, indicating that industry betas might prove better in practical use than individual company betas. Another factor which might suggest use of industry betas is that many companies are multi-activity, i.e. they are themselves diversified. Therefore their ungeared equity beta will itself be a weighted average of a number of project betas and might not be appropriate for use in project appraisal.

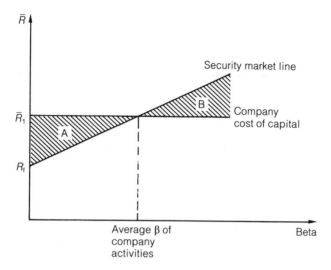

Fig. 6.1. CAPM compared with single cost of capital.

CAPM and single company cost of capital

Figure 6.1 compares decisions made using CAPM and the security market line with decisions made using a single company cost of capital. CAPM provides a forward-looking project-based variable rate decision where the required rate is related to risk as measured by beta. A single company cost of capital will tend to be an average rate of return reflecting the current average risk level of the company and not necessarily relating to the risk of the project under review. Use of a single cost of capital could lead to the rejection of low-risk viable projects located in shaded area A while accepting high-risk projects failing to earn an adequate rate of return and located in area B. A single company cost of capital may also reflect the financing policy of the company (e.g. if a weighted average cost of capital is used) and thus the cost mixes together project and financial risk. Use of a project beta will allow the project to be assessed on its own and then any financing side effects could be valued separately. This adjusted present value approach is discussed in Chapter 11.

CAPM, diversification and smaller companies

Does diversification add value to companies? The answer to this is that diversification *per se* should not, under the theory examined, add value. Shareholders can diversify, and indeed are assumed to have diversified away all non-market risk. Therefore diversification by companies is mere duplication. However, if companies can add value by buying other companies this is different; in this case, diversification is a consequence of a profitable deal rather than the cause of the profit.

Diversification makes more sense from a managerial perspective and this could be the motivation. It may also be argued that it is valuable for smaller companies where owner managers have substantial amounts of their own wealth invested in the company. In our example we used quoted company data to compute a required return for an unquoted company. Was this valid? It could be argued that as all businesses are competing in the same product market then the equilibrium rate of return will be the same for all. This would justify the use of a universal asset/ project beta. However, there is evidence to suggest that smaller companies have, on average, provided higher risk-adjusted returns than larger companies. This is discussed as an efficient market anomaly in Chapter 8. This has led to suggestions that investors might require higher returns from smaller companies (a smaller companies risk premium) and that this should be reflected in managers' project appraisal. There are thus conflicting views. Perhaps a solution would be to use the market determined asset/project rate of return and then carry out a sensitivity analysis (Chapter 7) with higher rates to see how crucial the discount rate is to the viability of the project.

Factors determining betas

The stability of betas was referred to in earlier discussions and one reason for equity betas changing over time might relate to factors affecting beta values. These factors include

1. The way in which project/activity returns relate to mainstream economic activity. If a project's returns are highly correlated with mainstream activity it will be likely to have a high beta. If this relationship changed over time the beta value would tend to change also.
2. The proportion of fixed costs in the cost structure of the project will also affect the beta value. This is analogous to the effect that debt has on the equity beta. Fixed costs have to be paid irrespective of the level of goods produced and therefore a high proportion of fixed costs will normally be associated with a high project beta. Changes in cost structure could therefore lead to changes in the beta value.
3. The type of business activity a company is engaged in will affect the value of its equity beta. If this business activity changes or the mix changes in a multi-activity company, then beta is likely to change as well.
4. The effect of financial gearing on equity betas has already been discussed. Obviously changes in the level of financial gearing will reflect in the value of the equity beta.

CAPM problems and a possible successor

Although CAPM can be criticized it has nevertheless provided a theory which has been the basis of a practical approach to risk in evaluating financial securities and the risk of undertaking business activities. It is by no means perfect and it is valid to question whether risk can be represented by just a single factor, beta. The problem of applying an *ex ante* single-period theory to multi-period projects where historic data are used to obtain risk measures is a further issue. The composition of the market portfolio used in testing CAPM has also been criticized. The theoretical market portfolio is composed of all risky assets world-wide, whereas in practice the proxy portfolios used tend to be security market indices relating to a single country. However, CAPM has been used for some years now and continues to be a popular approach to defining risk.

A successor to CAPM could be the Arbitrage Pricing Model (APM) developed by Ross. This model is more general than CAPM and assumes that each security's return depends on a number of independent factors rather than just one. With APM the expected return $\bar{E}$ on a security could be written as

$$\bar{E} = R_f + b_1(F_1 - R_f) + b_2(F_2 - R_f) \ldots$$

where R_f is the risk-free rate of return, F_1, F_2 etc. are the expected returns on portfolios with unit sensitivity to factor 1, factor 2 etc. and no sensitivity to any other factor, while b_1, b_2 etc. are the sensitivity of the individual security to changes in the factors.

APM is thus a multi-factor model and research undertaken in the USA suggested that the four most important factors were: unanticipated inflation, changes in the expected level of industrial production, changes in the default risk premium on bonds and unanticipated changes in the term structure of interest rates.

7   Risk analysis

Introduction

In the previous two chapters a theory of risk was developed which could be used in determining the differing levels of risk and return inherent in different types of business activity. In this context, risk was related to the risk faced by investors in financial markets. In this chapter we examine techniques of risk analysis which are not based on any generalized theory of risk but enable decision makers to gain insights of varying kinds into factors affecting investment returns.

Payback period

In Chapters 2 and 3 the use of payback in project appraisal was discussed. The payback period is the time taken to recoup the initial investment outlay. A full discussion on payback is given in Chapter 3. Although the payback period can be criticized as a method of project appraisal it is often used in conjunction with other methods (e.g. NPV or IRR). It is said that this adds another piece of information to be used in the decision-making process. For example there may be a horizon date after which it is felt the business environment becomes much less certain. An example of this might be investment in Hong Kong where sovereignty is to be transferred in 1997. A further refinement is to use discounted payback where the payback period is calculated using discounted cash flow values. It is said that this helps partly to answer one of the criticisms of payback by taking into account the time value of money and timing of cash flows.

Sensitivity analysis

The use of sensitivity analysis enables decision makers to identify those factors to which the project may be most vulnerable. It is usually used in conjunction with NPV or IRR computations. Holding all other factors constant each factor is varied in turn to find out the impact on project NPV or IRR. A number of approaches can be used; pessimistic and optimistic forecasts could be used for each variable; the amount by which each variable could change and the project just break even could be calculated; alternatively, more than one variable at a time could be altered and the effect on project NPV/IRR calculated. The application of sensitivity analysis is simplified by using a standard PC spreadsheet package.

Sensitivity analysis can be better understood with the help of an example.

Example

For an investment project, the following tentative initial estimates have been made:

			Sales volumes
Outlay	£100 000		
Sales price	£30	Year 1	4000 units
Unit cost	£20	Year 2	6000 units
Discount rate	10% p.a.	Year 3	3000 units
Life	3 years		

The £100 000 purchases equipment which will manufacture a product produced at the above unit cost and selling at the sales price in the volumes indicated.

1. Calculate the maximum tolerable unfavourable change (as a percentage of the original estimated value) in
   (a) sales price;
   (b) unit cost;
   (c) sales volume;
   (d) initial outlay;
   (e) discount rate;
   (f) project lifetime.
   Comment on the results. Could the sales volumes be treated *separately* in the analysis?
2. Now suppose that government anti-inflation policy will allow sales prices to rise by 10% p.a. compound but unit costs are expected to rise at an annual rate of 20% compound (both starting at $t = 0$). What initial cash subsidy would be necessary to retain viability for the project?

Solution

With sales price p, unit cost c, and sales volume v, in any year the net revenue will be R where

$$R = v(p - c)$$

Thus in the first year of the project where $p = 30$, $c = 20$ and $v = 4000$ the revenue will be 40 000. On the basis of the original estimates the cash flows will be $-100\,000$; 40 000; 60 000; 30 000; so that net present value will be:

$$NPV = -100\,000 + \frac{40\,000}{1.1} + \frac{60\,000}{1.21} + \frac{30\,000}{1.331} = 8490$$

Thus the project is worthwhile. Now if the revenues changed in such a way that gross present value came down from 108 490 to 100 000 the project would break even with zero NPV. Now although the revenues are unequal in the three years they will all be affected in *equal proportion* by a change in v or a change in $(p - c)$. In particular if the value of $p - c$ was halved to five then GPV would be halved. Similarly if $p - c$ was replaced by:

$$\frac{100\,000}{108\,490}(p - c)$$

then GPV would be 100 000; giving zero NPV. If c remains constant at 20, then if p was such that the margin was

$$\frac{100\,000 \times 10}{108\,490}$$

then NPV would be zero. Thus p must be such that the margin is 9.22. The minimum value of p, *ceteris paribus*, is 29.22. This represents a fall of 0.78 or just 2.60%. On the other hand, given $p = 30$, the value of c required to give a margin of 9.22 is 20.78, which would represent a rise of 3.90%.

In respect of sales volume, if each year was affected in the same proportion and if all volume figures stood at

$$\frac{100\,000}{108\,490} \times 100\%$$

of the original values, then NPV would be zero. Thus the requisite percentage fall in v is

$$\frac{8490}{108\,490} \times 100\% = 7.83\%$$

If GPV remains at 108 490 then the initial outlay must not exceed this figure. Obviously this would represent a rise of 8.49%.

The discount rate at which the project would just break even is, by definition, the IRR/yield. Thus, setting

$$-100\,000 + \frac{40\,000}{1 + r} + \frac{60\,000}{(1 + r)^2} + \frac{30\,000}{(1 + r)^3} = 0$$

and solving for r gives a value of 0.149 or 14.9%. The discount rate could thus rise by 4.9 or 49% and the project would just break even.

In analysing the effects of variation in the project's lifetime we start by considering the present values if the project only ran for two years. This would be

$$\text{NPV (2 years)} = -100\,000 + \frac{40\,000}{1.1} + \frac{60\,000}{1.21} = 14\,050$$

Thus for viability the project needs to run for such a part of the third year that the present value of the part return is 14 050; which would bring NPV up to zero level. A fairly plausible assumption about happenings in the third year is that if the project runs for some fraction, f, of the year, then the return achieved will be 30 000 f and the timing of the return would be after $2 + f$ years. Thus we require that f be such that

$$\frac{30\,000f}{(1.1)^{2+f}} = 14\,050$$

A trial-and-error procedure produced the following results:

f	$\dfrac{30\,000f}{(1.1)^{2+f}}$
0.70	16 235
0.65	15 148
0.60	14 049 ←
0.61	14 270

A value of 0.70 was guessed for f to begin with, but this would give too high (14 050 is the required figure) a result for the present value. The right value of f turned out to be 0.60 as indicated by the arrow in the table. Thus, on the basis of the assumptions made, if the project ran for 2.6 years instead of three years then break-even would be achieved. This would represent a reduction in lifetime of 13.33%.

The results in total are presented in the following table:

Factor	Variation (%)
Price	2.60
Unit cost	3.90
Sales volume	7.83
Outlay	8.49
Discount rate	49.0
Lifetime	13.33

We could conclude from this that the project is sensitive to all factors except discount rate but particularly so in respect of price and cost. If, as is often the case, these are volatile parameters, the viability of the project could easily be jeopardized. Of course, we cannot specify a particular percentage variation, in general, which represents the boundary point for sensitivity. An arbitrary, but informed, decision has to be made in the light of particular cases. However, judging by typical payback periods in practice anything below 20 or 30% would be regarded as sensitive.

Sales volumes in the individual years can easily be examined. For instance, assuming that everything is as originally estimated in years 2 and 3, and that sales volume in year 1 is v_1 then v_1 must be such as to produce zero NPV. Thus

$$\frac{10v_1}{1.1} + \frac{60\,000}{1.21} + \frac{30\,000}{1.331} = 100\,000$$

This equation solves for $v_1 = 3066$, a reduction of 23.35%. For year 2 the equation is

$$\frac{40\,000}{1.1} + \frac{10v_2}{1.21} + \frac{30\,000}{1.331} = 100\,000$$

which solves for $v_2 = 4973$, a reduction of 17.12%. Finally, for year 3:

$$\frac{40\,000}{1.1} + \frac{60\,000}{1.21} + \frac{10v_3}{1.331} = 100\,000$$

solves for $v_3 = 1870$, a reduction of 37.67%. It would appear then that the project is most sensitive to sales performance in the second year, and least sensitive in the third year.

Now consider the inflation scenario. The calculations necessary to ascertain present value are shown in the following table:

t	p	c	$p - c$	R	pv
1	33.0	24.00	9.00	36 000	32 727.27
2	36.30	28.80	7.50	45 000	37 190.08
3	39.93	34.56	5.37	16 110	12 103.68
					82 021.03

It will be seen that the margin starts to decline at once and in increasing absolute amounts. The gross present value plunges to 82.021. Therefore, a subsidy sufficient to bring this figure up to 100 000 would be needed for economic viability. Thus the subsidy required would be 17 979.

The example shows how sensitivity to changes in various factors can be calculated. This information as shown in the table can be used in a number of ways.

The decision makers will be able to take the sensitivity analysis into account in making their decision and if the project's success depends on one or a number of factors where only a small percentage change would lead to a negative outcome they might decide not to proceed with the project. Alternatively the decision makers could identify the most vulnerable factors and review their original forecasts for these factors increasing, if possible, their reliability. Finally, management may decide to go ahead with the project, but having had their attention drawn to vulnerable factors may make contingency plans based on the information obtained.

A drawback of the sensitivity analysis illustrated is that the factors were varied only one at a time. In reality there may be interdependencies; for example, changes in sales volume might be accompanied by changes in sales price. As mentioned earlier it may be possible to use a spreadsheet package and a PC to carry out analyses where more than one factor is altered at a time and the affect on NPV measured. A further problem will be in estimating how various factors might vary when changes occur. As more and more combinations of changes are considered we move nearer to a full simulation which is discussed in the following section.

Despite the simplicity of sensitivity analysis it is nevertheless a useful and often-used method of project analysis, even with major projects using sophisticated methods of project appraisal.

Simulation

Unlike sensitivity analysis, Monte Carlo simulation enables the decision maker to consider all possible combinations of the factors affecting the

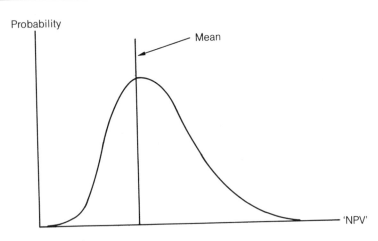

Fig. 7.1. Distribution of NPVs.

project under review. The use of simulation requires that a probability distribution of each of the variables affecting cash flows is known. Monte Carlo simulation, as its name suggests, is based on random sampling of the various distributions of variables and using them to compute an NPV for each sample. Using a computer, this process is repeated many times so that a dependable distribution of NPVs is obtained. The mean and variance of the distribution can then be estimated and represented as in Fig. 7.1.

Figure 7.1 shows how the distribution of NPVs for a project would be represented and also indicates the mean NPV. The results of simulation can be made available to decision makers to help them assess the return and risk of projects.

The discount rate used in simulation is interesting. Most writers advise using the risk-free rate rather than any risk-adjusted rate of return. The argument is that by using the risk-free rate the prejudgment of risk is avoided and the decision maker can base his assessment of risk on the distribution of NPVs and variance thereof obtained by the simulation and as illustrated in Fig. 7.1. A counter argument would be that while use of the risk-free rate might be justified in a perfect (or near perfect) market scenario, appraisal of projects in an uncertain scenario should make use of differential rates as discussed in the previous chapter. A way round the discount rate problem and one used in many appraisals is to compute a distribution of IRRs and the mean and variance of such a distribution. Decision makers can then be presented with a diagram similar to that shown in Fig. 7.1 except it will represent IRRs rather than NPVs.

The use of simulation is appealing but it is demanding both on analysts' and computer time. However, the modelling process required to undertake simulation can itself be useful as it requires more detailed analysis of the project than might otherwise be undertaken. A criticism of this approach is that it is not always clear what a distribution of NPVs, or for that matter IRRs means. As stated in the introduction to this chapter, these techniques have no theoretical rationale and the decision maker has to make his own decisions on the relationship (if any!) between mean and variance of the NPVs/IRRs obtained.

Single project risk analysis

There are a number of ways in which probabilistic data relating to a single project can be analysed and presented to management to aid decision making. The starting point for the analysis, given a discrete probability distribution of the returns in each year, is the idea of expected net present value (ENPV). This is given by

$$\text{ENPV} = \sum_{t=0}^{n} \bar{R}_t(1 + r)^{-t}$$

where $\bar{R}_t$ is the expected (arithmetic mean) cash flow return in year t. R_0 represents initial outlay. No investors are assumed to be return averse so greater ENPV's are preferred to lesser. In the full probabilistic description of a project risk profiles can be produced showing the chance that NPV will exceed any given level. Similar results can be produced for yield.

Overall dispersion of NPV is important. This is measured by standard deviation (or variance) of NPV given by

$$\sigma_{\text{NPV}} = \sqrt{\Sigma p(\text{NPV} - \text{ENPV})^2}$$

Less dispersion is preferred to greater (for a given mean return). σ_{NPV} is a 'proxy' measure of total risk on an investment. Mutually offsetting variations must be taken into account when more than one project is involved.

The coefficient of variation, the ratio of σ_{NPV} to ENPV, is a measure of relative, rather than absolute, dispersion. The coefficient of variation can be interpreted as a risk measure or, in certain circumstances, as an overall criterion for acceptability. Managers can make comparisons between projects' risk-return payoffs based on relative coefficients of variation; alternatively a minimum acceptable coefficient figure could be determined as part of the project screening process.

The variance of net present value can be expressed in terms of the variances of and covariances between, individual cash flow items. Variance (σ_{NPV}^2) is given by

$$\sigma_{\text{NPV}}^2 = \sum_{t=0}^{n} \text{Var}(R_t)(1 + r)^{-2t} + \sum_{\substack{S=0 \\ S \neq t}} \sum_{t=0} \text{Cov}(R_s, R_t)(1 + r)^{-(S+t)}$$

in the most general case for an individual project.

A number of interesting special cases emerge. For uncorrelated returns:

$$\sigma_{\text{NPV}}^2 = \sum_{t=0}^{n} \text{Var}(R_t)(1 + r)^{-2t}$$

and in the case of perfectly positively correlated returns:

$$\sigma^2_{\text{NPV}} = \left[\sum_{t=0}^{n} V(R_t)(1 + r)^{-t} \right]$$

We will now examine a worked example illustrating the calculation of these measures.

Example

An investment proposal has the following probability distribution of returns:

Year 1		Year 2		Year 3	
Return	Probability	Return	Probability	Return	Probability
6000	0.2	8 000	0.5	7 000	0.3
8000	0.4	12 000	0.5	11 000	0.5
9000	0.4			17 000	0.2

The events of each year are independent of other years. The outlay on the project is fixed at 22 000 and the appropriate discount rate figure is 10%. Find:

1. the expected net present value;
2. the variance of return in each of the years;
3. the standard deviation of net present value;
4. the coefficient of variation.

Solution

1. The expected net present value (ENPV) is the present value of the expected returns in each year, i.e.

$$\text{ENPV} = \sum_{t=0}^{n} \bar{R}_t (1 + r)^{-t}$$

In this case the outlay is fixed at 22 000 so that $R_0 = -22\,000$. The expected return in year 1, R_t, is 8000. The workings are

Return (R)	Probability (p)	pR
6000	0.2	1200
8000	0.4	3200
9000	0.4	3600
		8000

and the expected returns in years 2 and 3 are (by similar arithmetic mean calculations) found to be $R_2 = 10\,000$ and $R_3 = 11\,000$. Thus ENPV is given by

$$\text{ENPV} = -22\,000 + \frac{8000}{(1.1)} + \frac{10\,000}{(1.21)} + \frac{11\,000}{(1.331)} = 1801.65$$

2. Now variance of return in any year t is given by:

$$\text{Var } R_t = \Sigma p_t (R_t - \bar{R}_t)^2$$

So that for year 1 the workings are (with $\bar{R}_1 = 8000$)

Return (R_t)	Probability (p_t)	$R_t - \bar{R}_t$	$(R_t - \bar{R}_t)^2$	$p(R_t - \bar{R}_t)^2$
6000	0.2	−2000	4 000 000	800 000
8000	0.4	0	0	0
9000	0.4	1000	1 000 000	400 000

$$\text{Var } R_1 = 1\,200\,000$$

3. We are told in the question that there is independence between years; that is, covariances are zero. Thus since variance of outlay is zero, applying the equation for uncorrelated returns:

$$\sigma^2_{NPV} = 0 + \frac{1\,200\,000}{(1.1)^2} + \frac{4\,000\,000}{(1.1)^4} + \frac{12\,000\,000}{(1.1)^6}$$

$$= 10\,497\,476.52$$

$$\therefore \sigma_{NPV} = 3\,239.98$$

4. The coefficient of variation is the ratio of standard deviation – an absolute measure of dispersion – to arithmetic mean. Thus

$$c = \frac{3\,239.98}{1\,801.65} = 1.7983$$

The figures computed for ENPV, σ_{NPV} and c can then be used by the decision maker either on their own or in comparison with similar measures for other projects.

8 Market efficiency

Introduction

The existence of efficient capital markets has important implications both for investors in those markets and for companies obtaining finance through the markets. As we shall see, prices in efficient markets are reliable in that they reflect available information and can therefore be used as the basis of transactions between firms requiring funds and those willing to provide such funds.

To understand the concept of efficient capital markets it is useful to contrast them with perfect capital markets. The following conditions are necessary for perfect capital markets:

1. Markets are frictionless; there are no transaction costs or taxes; all assets are perfectly divisible and marketable.
2. There is perfect competition in product and securities markets.
3. Markets are informationally efficient, that is information is costless and is received simultaneously by all individuals.
4. All individuals are rational expected utility maximizers.

Given these conditions product and security markets will be both allocationally and operationally efficient. A market is said to be allocationally efficient when prices are determined in a way which equates marginal rates of return for all producers and savers. In such a market scarce savings are optimally allocated to productive investments in a way which benefits everyone. Operational efficiency deals with the cost of transferring funds; in the ideal world of perfect capital markets transaction costs are assumed to be zero and therefore we have perfect operational efficiency.

Capital market efficiency is much less restrictive than the notion of perfect capital markets outlined above. In an efficient capital market prices fully and instantaneously reflect all available relevant information. This means that when assets are traded prices are accurate signals for capital allocation. Stock market efficiency therefore is concerned with information and pricing efficiency.

To illustrate the difference between perfect markets and efficient capital markets we can relax some of the perfect market assumptions. We can still have efficient capital markets if markets are not frictionless, prices will still fully reflect all available information if, for example, brokerage fees have to be paid. It is important to note that there can be imperfect competition in product markets while we still have efficient capital markets. Therefore a firm could make monopoly profits in the product market but the efficient capital market will determine a share price which fully reflects the expected present value of the monopoly profits. It is therefore possible to have allocative inefficiencies in product markets but still have efficient capital markets.

Three types of market efficiency are defined in the literature based on what type of information is being considered. These are as follows:

1. **Weak form efficiency.** This says that no investor can earn above average returns by developing trading rules based on historical price or return information. This would seem to rule out the activities of, for example, technical analysts.
2. **Semi-strong form efficiency.** This says that no investor can be expected to earn above average returns from trading rules based on any publicly available information. This casts doubt on investors' ability to trade profitably as a result of publicly available information obtained from the annual reports of companies and similar sources.
3. **Strong form efficiency.** This is saying that no investor can earn above average returns using any information, whether publicly available or not.

The last type of market efficiency is extremely powerful. If markets were efficient in their strong form then prices would fully reflect all information even though it was held exclusively by a company insider. The usual assumption is that insiders could earn excess returns by trading on the basis of their privileged information, but if they did so they would be operating outside the law and liable to prosecution.

The concept of market efficiency has aroused considerable controversy, not least because it casts doubt on the ability of professional investment analysts to select securities which will produce above average returns. The theory has been subjected to a continuous series of tests which still and will continue. These tests follow the type of market efficiency outlined above.

Testing market efficiency

Weak form tests
Weak form tests can be categorized under two main headings:

1. Those which seek to determine the degree of independence of successive share prices and/or indices. In these tests, series of share prices or indices are subjected to statistical tests to determine whether there is any correlation between past and present prices, that is by examining a series of past prices is it possible to predict what prices are going to be in the future. The weight of evidence suggests that it is not possible to predict future prices by looking at a series of past prices.

2. Trading rules. These tests try and determine whether it is possible by following standardized trading rules to earn an above average rate of return. Such rules might be of the form: 'Buy following a fall of $x\%$; sell when the price has risen $y\%$'.

Evidence to date largely supports the weak form market efficiency. However, attention is drawn to the research undertaken on changes occurring during the course of the trading day. Daily prices tended to be the minimum time period used in most of the earlier tests and it could be that by considering hourly or shorter changes that some inefficiencies might be discovered. There do in fact seem to be a number of anomolies that have been identified. These are discussed under the heading of anomalies below. Care must be taken in interpreting anomalies as their significance depends upon whether they present opportunities for profitable trading after transaction costs.

Semi-strong form tests
These tests seek to establish whether above average returns can be realized by trading in securities on the release of new information. Examples of the type of information which has been used in the tests are stock splits, information relating to mergers and takeovers, and accounting information contained in the companies' financial statements. Again the evidence tends to support the semi-strong form of market efficiency. Prices react rapidly to new information, therefore removing the opportunity for profitable trading. However, anomalies have been identified, particularly in connection with the returns earned on smaller companies and these are discussed under size effect below.

Strong form tests
A number of tests categorized under this heading have examined whether any investors can consistently earn superior risk-adjusted returns. The assumption is that because of superior knowledge and skills professional portfolio managers, e.g. unit trust and pension fund managers, should be able to earn above average returns. The evidence suggests that although some managers do indeed earn such returns they do not do so consistently and the good performance of some is compensated by poor performance by others. However, there is evidence that insiders having access to privileged information can obtain superior returns by dealing in securities where they know more or better information than market participants generally. This is evidence of strong form inefficiency. However, insider-trading is illegal and rigorous application of the law should help provide markets fair to all.

Market anomalies

Although broad support for market efficiency has been obtained from testing the weak and semi-strong forms a number of anomalies have been identified. It should be stressed that any test is only a test of that piece of information in that particular market at that particular time. Results are not transferable over time or between markets; however, if an anomaly persists it means that a continuing opportunity is available to earn above average returns, provided of course that these excess returns are not dissipated by transaction costs. The normal expectation would be that in a competitive market, excess profits would be traded away once all market participants became aware of the anomaly.

Timing anomalies

Anomalies have been identified in that above average returns were earned for trading at certain times of the day, certain days of the week and certain months of the year.

It was found in the USA that the first 45 minutes of trading on Mondays produced negative returns, while on other weekdays there were positive returns. It was also found that prices rose on all weekdays in the last 15 minutes of trading. No convincing reasons for the anomalies appear to have been advanced.

Researchers also identified that below average returns were made from trading on Mondays. An explanation suggested for this is that investors review their investments at the weekend and initiate sell decisions on Mondays. However, buy decisions are deferred until later in the week as they are usually initiated by brokers. Another suggestion is that part of the explanation is due to the dates of settlement periods. Neither sounds entirely convincing.

It was also found that higher returns were made from trading in January in the USA and in April in the UK. The most popular explanation for this anomaly has been attributed to tax-loss selling. Investors with losses on shares have an incentive to sell at the end of the tax year so that the losses can be offset against gains made thus reducing their tax liability. The tax year ends in December in the US and March in the UK. Thus share prices will be depressed in these months due to tax-loss selling, but will tend to rebound in the following month, giving opportunities for superior returns.

Size anomalies

Research in both the US and the UK has shown that over a long-run period of several years, investing in smaller companies produces significantly higher returns than would be expected; in the US, smaller firms outperformed others by 4% p.a. compound, in the UK by 6% p.a. Why should this be? It has been suggested that the smaller size of the companies makes faster growth easier; however, if investors thought that this was the case prices would reflect the higher growth potential. A possible partial explanation is that smaller companies are inherently more risky than larger companies and that risk has been understated in computing the small company returns. This is a possibility but unlikely to explain the size or persistence of the effect. It has been questioned whether such large excess gains could be made when dealing costs and spread are considered. Again a possibility, but is excessive trading necessary to obtain excess returns? The size anomaly remains largely unexplained; however, recent returns (in 1989 and 1990) on small companies have been disappointing as their performance has been poor in comparison to larger companies.

Over-reaction to new information

Recent work in the US suggests that there is a tendency for investors to overweight recent information. This can cause a short-run departure from intrinsic values if, for example, prices bounce too high on the release of unexpected good news about the company. This was found in the US where there was over-reaction to short-term earnings movements. Unfortunately this is bad news for managers seeking to maximize shareholders' welfare by adopting long-term wealth-maximizing projects. Such projects may take time to reflect in conventional earnings figures leading to short-term underperformance of share price if too much emphasis is placed on current earnings figures. A by-product of the over-reaction syndrome is increasing volatility of share prices.

Implication of efficient markets theory

Investment/portfolio managers

The existence of efficient markets does not mean that investment research can be abandoned. As a number of writers have pointed out, it is only the competing work of analysts that keeps the market efficient. However, there may be scope for less traditional fundamental analysis with additional efforts being made to interpret information in different and unique ways in order to obtain new and more unconventional insights.

If the identification of superior individual securities seems to be largely a fruitless task then the investment advisor needs to concentrate on other aspects:

1. The level of risk should be that desired by or appropriate to the fund clientele.
2. Transaction costs should be reduced by not switching securities unnecessarily. Some fund managers are accused of 'churning' their portfolio without achieving a superior performance. Investment managers sometimes face something of a dilemma over switching securities as clients may think that they are not doing a good job if they do not periodically make such switches.
3. An important factor to consider could be the tax status of the investor. Investors with high marginal rates of personal tax may have different requirements than those with zero or nil rates of tax.

It should finally be pointed out that most of the tests relating to market efficiency have been carried out in the United Kingdom and the United States. It should not automatically be assumed that results obtained in these two countries can be transferred to all other countries with capital markets. The UK and USA contain large numbers of sophisticated investors and information is available to everyone more or less at the same time due to the excellent means of communication. In some countries the market might be dominated by a small number of wealthy individuals or corporations and, in addition, the dissemination of information, which is crucial to market efficiency, might be less than perfect.

Corporate financial managers

If markets are truly efficient, then it means that security prices are fair prices and both managers within companies and investors can feel confident in transacting business at prevailing market prices.

Timing share issues

Picking a 'best time' to issue shares should be an impossible and time-wasting task. Prices will reflect all information relating to the company. However, if managers know information that has not yet been released to the market (strong form inefficiency) they will be in a position to gauge whether current prices under or over-value the company. Although the timing of an issue should not matter, the existence of asymmetries of information in the market may lead to managers choosing to issue shares before bad news is released which will depress share prices. If the market believes that new share issues are more likely to be made when managers are in possession of bad news this would explain share price declines on the announcement of a new issue. In theory though the timing of new issues should be irrelevant.

Pricing acquisitions

Takeover bids are sometimes launched at prices well in excess of current target share values. To justify such bids, predator company directors must identify potential increases in value not already anticipated by the market and incorporated in the share price. Unless this can be done the predator will be paying over the price for a market-traded item. Of course, because the future is uncertain the bid could still turn out to be highly successful, but equally it could turn out to be a disaster. This helps explain the modest results relating to gains by predator company shareholders in mergers and acquisitions.

Creative accounting

Many tests of semi-strong market efficiency have examined whether market prices are affected by changes in accounting policy. In these situations companies may be merely changing presentation so that key figures and ratios appear to be better, but the underlying position remains unchanged, or there may be economic consequences, e.g. a change in the amount or timing of tax payments. The results seem to indicate that the market is not fooled by cosmetic changes; analysts are able to interpret the significance of any changes and market prices tend to react only if the information relates to unexpected changes in the predicted cash flows of the company. However companies, or more accurately their directors and advisors, continue to try and devise ever more sophisticated schemes for improving profit figures and balance sheet figures, does it matter? The answer seems to be that provided there is full disclosure somewhere the market will not be fooled; however, if ways are found of concealing information it is likely that the market will be misled even if this is only a short-term situation.

9 Equity share capital

Introduction

Limited liability companies have a number of features distinguishing them from unincorporated business enterprises:

1. A limited company has an existence and legal identity quite distinct from its members.
2. It follows from (1) that the company continues perpetually in existence irrespective of changes in its membership.
3. Members do not contractually bind the company. Management is carried out by the directors. Except in smaller companies, this leads to a division between ownership and management.
4. Company activities are more constrained. The scope of activities is limited by the memorandum of association and the Companies Act provide provisions regulating many aspects of operation and management.
5. Finally, but crucially, the liability of members is limited to any amount unpaid on called-up capital.

Types of company

The Companies Act 1985 distinguishes between

1. **Public companies**
   (a) Can be formed by two persons.
   (b) Limited by shares with a share capital.
   (c) Name of company ends with 'Public Limited Company' (PLC).
   (d) States in memorandum of association that it is a public company.
   (e) Authorized minimum share capital £50 000.
   (f) Can offer shares to public.
2. **Private companies**
   (a) Can be formed by two persons.
   (b) Limited by shares or guarantee with a share capital.
   (c) Name of company ends with 'Limited' (Ltd).
   (d) Cannot offer shares to public but can make offer to limited group.

A company's activities are regulated by its memorandum and articles of association. The **memorandum** deals with the relationship between the company and the outside world and must state

1. company's name;
2. whether it is public or private;
3. situation of registered office;
4. objects of the company;
5. if company has a share capital, amount of capital and number of shares.

The **articles of association** regulate the rights of members of a company between themselves and would include clauses on

1. share capital and variation of rights;
2. transfer of shares and alteration of capital;
3. meetings and voting rights of members;
4. appointment, powers, duties and removal of directors;
5. annual accounts, profits and dividends;
6. winding-up of the company.

Share capital

Equity share capital is often referred to as 'risk capital'. This is because it stands at the end of the line when payments of dividends and, in the event of winding-up, capital are made. However, it could also be looked on as 'reward capital' as it is entitled to all residual profits after prior fixed claims have been met.

The main features of **equity capital** are:

1. Effectively perpetual investment as return of money only made on liquidation.
2. No fixed or guaranteed dividend payment.
3. Dividends depend upon existence of profits.
4. Entitled to residue of profits after prior fixed claims met.
5. Last to be repaid on liquidation.
6. Value depends on company performance and realization depends on existence of market in shares or finding willing buyer.
7. Very importantly, equity capital carries voting rights, which means that as a class they usually have control of the company at company meetings.

Nearly all equity share capital is in the form of ordinary shares and most companies will have just this one category of equity. However, some companies have more than one category of equity with important distinguishing characteristics with regard to profit sharing and voting rights. Examples are 'deferred', 'founders' and 'non-voting'. There are often historic reasons for the existence of these different forms of equity. However, the contemporary view is that equity shareholders' rights should be in direct proportion to their investment and few new companies include such differences. In addition a number of other companies have fully integrated different classes of equity.

Companies in the UK can now purchase their own shares. This has long been possible in the USA and elsewhere, but it was not until the 1981 Companies Act that UK companies were permitted to do so. That Act (now consolidated into the Companies Act 1985) laid down strict provisions to be observed by companies purchasing their own shares. This is a useful strategy to have available and might be used, for example, by a cash-rich company with few potential investment opportunities. However, there are tax regulations which effectively treat repurchase proceeds as distributions making this strategy more attractive to some groups (tax exempt funds such as pension funds) than others.

Preference shares form part of the share capital of the company but although holders can be viewed as part-owners they usually only receive a fixed amount of dividend. This dividend ranks before ordinary shareholders' but after debt holders'. Preference dividend is not paid if profits are not available; in many cases preference shares are cumulative and therefore all arrears have to be paid before ordinary shareholders can receive a dividend.

As a source of finance, preference shares have tended to decline in popularity over the last 20 years. Since the introduction of corporation tax in 1965 preference and ordinary share dividends have been paid out of after-tax profits, whereas debt interest is charged against pre-tax profits and can be deducted for corporation tax purposes. In fact, after 1965, many companies introduced schemes to convert preference shares into debentures because of the different tax treatment.

From the investors' viewpoint, preference shares are riskier than debentures and may also carry no redemption date (i.e. be irredeemable). However, preference shares do have one advantage to corporate investors in that the dividends count as 'franked' income. This means that the income can be offset against the holders' corporation tax liability. This explains why over 75% of preference shares are held by companies.

The UK capital market

The **UK Stock Exchange** is, arguably, the most important part of the web of markets constituting the UK capital market. Although we are principally concerned with UK equity issues it should be stressed that there are important markets in UK government securities and overseas companies.

Primary market activity involves the issue of new securities thus spreading the risk and enabling new money to come into the company. **Secondary market** activity occurs where existing investors sell to willing buyers. No new money goes into the company; it is just an exchange of money for shares by buyer and seller.

The London Stock Exchange provides three different markets for sales:

1. listed market (full listing);
2. Unlisted Securities Market (USM);
3. third market (recently merged with USM);
4. shares traded under Rule 535(2) — this was formerly Rule 163(2).

As companies grow in size it becomes more difficult for existing share-holders to provide all new equity required. In addition, providers of fixed interest capital might prefer to deal with quoted companies and offer keener rates of interest to them. Also, older shareholders with a high proportion of their total wealth invested in the company might welcome the opportunity to realize part of their holding and reinvest the proceeds in other companies, thus diversifying investment risk. There may also be tax reasons for shareholders wishing to realize some or all of their investment.

For these and other reasons companies may wish to obtain a quotation on the Stock Exchange. To obtain a **full listing** certain minimum require-ments have to be satisfied, including

1. market capitalization — minimum total value £500 000;
2. marketability — at least 25% of any class of securities in hands of public;
3. Stock Exchange rules — company must comply with Stock Exchange rules.

There are considerable economies of scale in raising funds through a full listing but the cost of raising small amounts is high. During the 1970s the number of companies seeking new quotations on the listed market fell. This led to more publicity being given by the Stock Exchange to Rule 163(2) and to the creation in 1980 of the USM.

Under Rule 163(2) (now 535(2)) the Stock Exchange, from the 1950s, has allowed members to deal on an occasional basis in shares of unlisted companies if prior approval is obtained. However, the Stock Exchange was concerned that this effectively created an unregulated market and, recognizing the need for a market in shares for medium-sized companies, launched the USM in November 1980.

The USM has proved very successful, over 400 companies having come to the market by 1988. Requirements for admission to the USM are less onerous as only 10% of a company's issued capital has to be made available and only a three year trading record required.

In addition to the markets provided by the Stock Exchange an active trade takes place in the over-the-counter market operated by licensed dealers in securities.

Prior to the deregulation of the Stock Exchange in 1986 ('Big Bang'), most of the trading activities were conducted on the floor of the Stock Exchange between jobbers who made markets in shares and traded on their own behalf and brokers who bought and sold shares on behalf of clients.

Following Big Bang a computerized system was introduced. SEAQ (Stock Exchange Automated Quotation) records and displays via com-puter terminals and VDUs prices at which market makers are prepared to deal in securities. This information is available in dealing rooms throughout the City and now all dealing takes place by telephone. Big Bang also brought an end to dual capacity (the need for brokers and jobbers) and now market makers can sell shares direct to the public. A further refinement has been the classification of shares according to marketability with the most marketable shares being classified as alpha with beta, gamma and delta signifying declining degrees of marketability. Size, turnover and number of market makers determine the classifications.

Raising equity capital

Company shares can be issued or existing shares sold to the public in a variety of ways. A rights issue is the most important method of issuing new shares and is discussed in the next section. Outlined below are the other main methods in which shares are made available to the public.

1. **Offer for sale**
   (a) Company offers shares to issuing house.
   (b) Issuing house offers shares to public via prospectus.
   (c) Usually shares offered belong to existing shareholders and if so no new money is raised; however, some new shares could also be issued.
   (d) Most popular method for companies obtaining full listing.
2. **Public issue**
   (a) Similar to offer for sale but offer made direct by company.
   (b) Less common, normally used by large well known companies.
3. **Placing**
   (a) Securities sold privately to clients of issuing house handling issue.
   (b) Some have to be made available to dealers to make market.
   (c) Costs lower than offer for sale.
   (d) May be used for smaller issues.
   (e) Most popular method for USM companies.
4. **Stock Exchange introduction**
   (a) Used when shares already quoted in UK or elsewhere or shares already widely held and quotation required.
   (b) No new money raised.
5. **Tender**
   (a) Shares offered to public who name price.
   (b) Company places minimum reserve price.
   (c) Issue price is highest that will dispose of all shares.
   (d) Advantageous where fixing of issue price very difficult.

Underwriters for a fee agree to buy shares not taken up by the public. This ensures the success of the share issue.

Rights issues

Rights issues are pre-emptive issues, that is they give existing shareholders the right to subscribe for new shares at a price usually some way below the current market value. The terms of the offer are that each existing shareholder can take up new shares in proportion to his existing holding in the company. If all shareholders were to take up their rights then each would own exactly the same proportion of shares in the company after the rights as they had before. A rights issue ensures that existing shareholders are treated fairly and do not suffer the dilution of interest which would arise if new shareholders were offered shares at a price below current market value.

In some cases existing shareholders will not wish to take up their rights, but provided the rights can be sold at a fair price through the market, no loss will be experienced by the existing shareholders. This is an important point because it means that in theory the issue price of a rights issue should not matter and thus the timing of the rights and the discount of issue price on current market price should not affect share-holder wealth.

Consider the following example. The ordinary shares of Walker PLC are quoted at 100p. A rights issue of one for four is announced with a subscription price of 80p per share. Stride holds 1000 shares and is therefore entitled to buy 250 new shares at 80p each. He will then hold 1250 shares and these shares should be worth the previous market value of the original holding plus the new funds invested:

1000 shares at 100p	1000
New funds: 250 at 80p	200
	£1200
Ex rights price	$\dfrac{£1200}{1250} = 96p$

If Stride was to do nothing his shares would fall in value from £1000 to £960. He must therefore either take up the rights issue himself or sell the rights to someone else. The rights will be worth the difference between the subscription price and the price of the shares after the rights issue:

Ex rights price	96p
Subscription price	80p
Value of one right	16p

If Stride was to sell all his rights entitlement, his wealth after the sale of rights would be

Value of original holding	1000 at 96p = 960
Sale of rights	250 at 16p = 40
	£1000

Therefore whether Stride takes up the issue or sells the whole, or part of the rights he is entitled to, he should not suffer any loss in wealth.

Rights issues are usually underwritten by a merchant bank. For a fee the bank agrees to buy any shares not taken up by the existing share-holders. This would happen if the share price fell below the subscription price by date of payment. Alternatively a 'deep-discount' rights issue could be made where the subscription price is set so far below current market value that the risk of non-subscription is neglible; thus under-writing costs of approximately $2\frac{1}{2}\%$ of issue proceeds could be saved. However, deep-discount issues are not as common as might be expected. They require more shares to be issued and if dividends per share are maintained at pre-rights levels they involve companies in greatly increased dividend payments.

The advantages and disadvantages of rights issues include the following:

1. **Advantages**
   (a) No dilution of existing shareholders interests because of pre-emptive nature of issue.
   (b) Can be issued at any state of stock market cycle.
   (c) As issue price is irrelevant, need/cost of underwriting issue could be eliminated/reduced.
   (d) Issue costs lower than other forms of equity issue.
2. **Disadvantages**
   (a) More expensive than retentions because of issue costs.
   (b) Shareholders may be called on to provide finance out of taxed dividend income.
   (c) Share prices may be marked down if market traders consider many shareholders will sell their rights.

The loss or gain to shareholders of dividend payments followed by rights issues will depend upon the system of corporation tax and the shareholders' marginal tax rate. Under the imputation system of corporation tax, shareholders with marginal rates lower than basic rate (e.g. pension funds) will gain from such a strategy, while those with marginal rates higher than basic rate will lose.

The reaction of the stock market to a rights issue announcement should depend upon the use to which the issue is to be put. An announcement that the issue is to be used for profitable expansion should increase the demand for shares, thus increasing the market value. On the other hand, if a more cautious announcement is made the market reaction might be to mark the price down. The point being made is that the share price should be affected by the use to which the funds are to be put rather than the rights issue *per se*.

If the rights issue is to be used to finance a project which will increase the market value of the firm, i.e. a project having a positive net present value, then this increase in value belongs to the existing shareholders and should be reflected in the price of shares in issue before the rights issue is made. This increase will then automatically be included in the price of rights should they be sold rather than exercised by the current holder.

Share appraisal

Dividends and **earnings** are important factors in appraising the value of shares. Some of the more common measurements used to help evaluate share price are given below.

Dividend yield

$$\text{Dividend yield} = \frac{\text{Dividend per share}}{\text{Share price}} \times 100$$

This formula measures the rate of return received as dividend income. An investor in ordinary shares will normally expect return to comprise dividend and capital gain.

Because shareholders pay different rates of income tax the dividend figure used in the yield is usually the amount an exempt (nil tax rate) shareholder would receive. It is the **gross dividend yield** which is shown in the financial pages of newspapers. Therefore the dividend per share figure actually paid has to be multiplied by 100/75 to give the gross equivalent. This assumes a basic rate of income tax of 25%.

Earnings per share

$$\text{Earnings per share} = \frac{\text{Earnings after tax and prior claims}}{\text{Number of ordinary shares in issue}}$$

The earnings figure is the amount available to ordinary shareholders after all charges (including interest, tax and preference dividends) but before payment of any ordinary dividend. Note that it is the number of shares, not their nominal value.

There are four methods of calculating earnings per share:

1. Nil method — assumes no dividend.
2. Net method — any unrelieved ACT deducted.
3. Maximum distribution (gross) method — Adds ACT set off on payment of all profits as dividends.
4. Full tax method — Assumes profits are taxed at rate of CT with no offset for capital allowances etc. This last method is likely to have even less significance than at present as the changes in allowances and rates take effect.

Note that methods (1) and (2) are in many cases identical. Method (2) is the figure used in the financial press. Method (3) has greatest significance when calculating dividend cover.

Dividend cover

$$\text{Dividend cover} = \frac{\text{Earnings per share}}{\text{Dividends paid per share}}$$

Note that the earnings figure usually used is the maximum distribution figure. This is because we want to know the cover available if all earnings were paid out as dividends. We therefore need to consider the ACT position.

Earnings yield

$$\text{Earnings yield} = \frac{\text{Earnings per share}}{\text{Share price}} \times 100$$

Price/earnings ratio

$$\text{Price/earnings ratio} = \frac{\text{Share price}}{\text{Earnings per share}}$$

The 'net' earnings figure is usually used in these calculations. The P/E ratio is used by analysts to assess shares. A high P/E (low earnings yield) indicates expected growth and/or low risk.

Pricing new issues is extremely difficult. Although the price will be fixed by reference to price and yields of similar quoted companies, no two companies are the same and in some cases there may be no near comparison available. Although the vendors would like the highest price possible it cannot be pitched too high because it must appeal both to underwriters and to the investing public. Ideally the promoters of the issue would like to fix the price to ensure a slightly over-subscribed issue with the quotation opening at a small but not excessive premium.

If a company is new to the market expected dividend yield may be set above and P/E ratio below existing similar seasoned issues. Where the nature of the business is unique or the future profits difficult to forecast an issue by tender might be chosen.

Other aspects of the share market

Scrip dividends are sometimes used as an alternative to cash dividends. The profit which would have been paid as a cash dividend is used to capitalize new shares which are added to existing shareholders' holdings. The company's cash flow benefits and the shareholder has a marketable asset. At one time no tax was paid on scrip dividends but now they are treated in the same way as cash dividends, both for paying companies and shareholders.

Scrip/capitalization of bonus issues occur when a company capitalizes past reserves in paying up unissued shares to be issued pro rata to existing shareholders. The shareholders have more shares but theoretically should be no better off financially.

Stock splits occur where the company divides up the existing shares into units of lower denomination. No additional amounts are capitalized. The main objective is to lower unit dealing price and increase marketability. A spin off might be that dividends are not reduced proportionally, leading to a higher total dividend.

Venture capital is the term applied to the equity financing needs of the smaller (usually unquoted) company. The newer small company has often found it difficult to satisfy its financing needs. It has not got a proven track record nor has it access to the same financial markets as larger companies. Now more institutions (e.g. 3I) are prepared to back these companies and there is encouragement for private investors via the Business Expansion Scheme.

Vendor placings

During 1982 the amount raised by rights issues declined. This was to some extent a reaction following the record amount raised in the previous year but may also have reflected some disaffection with the rights issue as a primary source of new funds manifested during 1984. Dissatisfaction with rights issues stemmed from the view, expressed in some quarters, that the method was both relatively expensive and inflexible:

1. Expensive because of
    (a) practice of setting issue price of new shares at a discount on market price increases servicing costs if dividends are maintained;
    (b) underwriting fees payable.
2. Inflexible because at the time the Bank of England system required issuing companies to join a queue so that new issues coming to the market were spread evenly throughout the year. This could be inconvenient if, for example, cash was required to fund an acquisition.

For these reasons companies sought to raise funds by other ways and avoid conventional rights issues. One method used in recent years has been to take over an investment trust by share swap and then liquidate the trust's portfolio. This method has been used mainly by smaller companies as institutions have expressed disapproval to larger companies raising money in this way.

A significant development has been the increased use of 'vendor placings' to finance acquisitions. Previously, companies wanting to raise new money equivalent to a relatively small proportion of their equity, say 10–15%, to finance a corporate acquisition have been able to do so by calling an extraordinary general meeting and seeking the approval of a majority of shareholders to suspend pre-emptive rights; the new equity was then placed with a small number of institutional investors. However, in November 1984 three companies, Ward White, Saatchi and Saatchi and Dee Corporation opted, with the approval of their shareholders, to take out over 30% of equity for vendor placing, thereby breaking the City tradition.

These deals were deemed to be advantageous to the management of buying companies from several viewpoints. At that stage the rights issue queue was long owing to the British Telecom issue: this was crucial as any delay in raising money could have endangered the success of the acquisition. In addition, because City interest was roused by an acquisition, the shares in these companies were buoyant following the placing, whereas in the wake of a rights issue market over-reaction may sometimes leave shares depressed for several months.

Vendor placings may, however, be to the disadvantage of the small investor, who is excluded from the expansion of the equity and therefore experiences a dilution of his holding — in direct contravention of the principle of equity. Furthermore, he has no effective redress, since the legal requirements have been fulfilled by the company — the institutions which command the majority of shareholding and can vote for an exemption from pre-exemption rights are generally the recipients of the subsequent placing, and need not suffer any dilution in their holdings.

The future of the rights issue could also be influenced by the structural changes post Big Bang in the City. Large securities firms exist capable of absorbing whole tranches of stock which could then be disposed of over time in line with the US model. However, there are significant differences between the US and UK systems which indicate that a wholesale adoption of US practices might be inappropriate. For example, the US objective is to avoid a discount on new shares that would damage the interests of their existing shareholders, an approach which does not matter under the UK system where shareholders have pre-emptive rights. In addition, personal shareholders account for two-thirds of the US equity market, against less than a third in the UK, and US investors have easier recourse to legal action to redress perceived injustices than in the UK. The US system also tends to deter companies from raising equity capital in a falling market, whereas the rights system, in theory, allows companies to raise capital at any stage in the cycle. Moreover, from a political stance the abolition of, or even a shift in emphasis away from, the rights issue towards vendor placings might seem to be at odds with the government's policy of encouraging broader personal share ownership.

10 Long-term debt finance

Introduction

Debt finance comes in a number of forms which have become increasingly varied in recent years. Debt finance differs from equity as follows:

1. It is debt and therefore takes preference in liquidation over equity.
2. It may be secured on assets of the company.
3. The rate of interest is usually fixed (although it may float by reference to some base rate).
4. Interest is payable whether profits are earned or not.
5. Interest payments are tax deductible.

In the 1970s, companies were reluctant to enter into long-term fixed interest commitments because interest rates were high reflecting higher rates of expected inflation. This led to innovations in the types of issues made.

The use of **index linked** securities was recommended by the Wilson Committee but although such issues are used by the Government there has been little interest from the private sector. With such issues the redemption value is increased in line with an inflation index as is the interest payment. There is therefore an open-ended commitment which private sector companies might not wish to tie themselves to.

Floating rate loans are now common. This arrangement can protect both lender and borrower when interest rates are volatile. Rather than the loan carrying a fixed rate of interest, the rate is tied to a market rate, e.g. six months interbank rate plus 2%. When the interbank rate changes so does the interest payable on the loan.

Deep discount and zero coupon bonds are also now more common. These are issues at a very large discount on redemption value and/or low or zero rate of interest. The return to the holder comes in the form of increasing capital value as the bond moves towards maturity. The hold can defer tax until a disposal is made. The issuer gains by not having pay out sums (or only small amounts) during the life of the bond, enhancing cash flow during the early life of the bond.

Debentures

The terms **debenture**, **bond** and **loan stock** tend to be used interchangeably when referring to a company's formal debt issues. A debenture is a written acknowledgement by a company of a debt. It may be unsecured (naked) but is more usually secured either on specific assets or by a floating charge on the assets. In the latter case the company can still deal in the assets.

A company may, or be required to, set up a sinking fund to repay the debentures. With such a fund, sufficient amounts currently are invested to provide, with interest earned, the amount required to redeem the debenture at maturity. Although debentures can be issued which do not have a repayment date and are therefore perpetual, they are virtually always issued with a named repayment date or dates between which they will be redeemed.

1. Debentures are usually issued in parcels of £100.
2. **Issue price** may be at a discount or premium.
3. **Coupon rate** is the stated rate of interest per £100.
4. **Market price** is the current traded market value.
5. **Redemption value** is the amount payable on redemption.
6. **Interest yield**, (Annual interest/Market price) × 100, is a measure of limited use as it does not consider any capital gain or loss arising to redemption and ignores the time value of money.
7. **Redemption yield** (r) is a measure of the total return obtained by solving for r in the equation with redemption taking place in year n:

$$\text{Market price} = \sum_{t=1}^{n} \frac{\text{Interest payment}}{(1 + r)^t} + \frac{\text{Redemption value}}{(1 + r)^n}$$

This is essentially an internal rate of return (IRR) calculation and gives an average rate of return over the life of the bond.

However, expected return is not necessarily based on the same rate every year and this problem is discussed in the section on term structure of interest rates below.

Bank borrowing

This has increased in importance as a source of long-term finance in the last ten years; prior to this, banks were regarded as sources of short to medium-term finance. This is due to the response of the clearing banks to criticism on lack of long-term borrowing facilities and borrowers' preference for competitive interest rates often based on a floating rate. The bank will usually require security on the company's assets or the directors of smaller companies may be required to give personal guarantees. A repayment schedule is usually agreed and sometimes a 'grace' period in the early years of the loan is granted to allow establishment of the business.

Long-term loans may also be obtained from other financial institutions. 3I is one of the best known specialist institutions. Advances range from £5000 to £2 million, occasionally more. Most advances are secured medium- or long-term loans, but some equity (minority) shares are purchased. This is a valuable source of funds for smaller companies who can obtain expansion funds without sacrificing control to new investors.

Maturity of borrowing

Should a company borrow short, medium or long term? Factors to be considered include

1. existing maturity structure of debt;
2. amount required;
3. use to which funds will be put;
4. current and expected level of interest rates.

Maturities will be structured so that there are regular maturities at reasonable intervals. Managers tend to match finance with the asset being acquired; fixed assets being financed by long-term funds, short-lived assets with short-term funds.

The **term structure of interest rates** refers to the different rates of interest demanded on loans of differing maturities. At any time the term structure is a function of investors' expectations regarding movement in interest rates over time. Expectations about future inflation will be an important factor determining rates of interest. If inflation is expected to be high for the next one to two years but then to decline, short-term rates may be higher than long-term. The more usual assumption is that long-term rates will be higher than short-term rates. This is because of the increasing uncertainty as time increases and the demand by lenders to be compensated for taking on extra risk.

Term structure theories include:

1. expectations hypothesis;
2. liquidity preference theory;
3. inflation uncertainty premium;
4. market segmentation.

Convertibles, warrants and options

We now discuss the characteristics and valuation of **convertibles, warrants** and **options**. As convertibles and warrants can both be evaluated as options we deal first with options, then with convertibles and warrants.

Options
Options and option theory have both become the subject of increasing attention in recent years. This was particularly associated with the establishment of a traded options market in Chicago in 1973. This enabled investors in the USA to buy and sell options in the same way as they traded in shares of companies. The amount of business transacted grew at a very fast rate and increasing attention was paid to options and their valuation.

Option transactions are now recognized as a legitimate part of a portfolio manager's strategy, but it has also been pointed out by a number of writers that financial managers spend considerable time in evaluating options in the form of corporate financing and investment problems.

Although option trading in shares has been conducted on the Stock Exchange in London for a considerable number of years, it was only in 1978 that a traded options market was established, which led to an increasing interest in options and option trading.

A **call option** gives the holder the right to buy a share at a specified price known as the **exercise price** on or before a specified date. In contrast a **put option** gives the holder the right to sell at a specified price on or before a specified date.

American and European options differ in that European options can only be exercised at expiry date whereas American options can be exercised any time up to and including expiry date. It should be noted that nearly all the analysis deals with European options which are easiest to handle and in addition initially ignore dividends.

The value of an option is a function of

1. Exercise price of option (EX);
2. Current price of share (P);
3. Short-term interest rate (r_f);
4. Time to expiry (T);
5. Variance of rate of return on stock (σ^2).

It should be noted that the value is not a function of the expected return on the share.

The value of a call option at the expiry date will simply be the lower of ($P - $ EX) or zero. Should the exercise price exceed the current price at expiry date the option will go unexercised and have zero value. It should be noted that options cannot have a negative value. Where the option has some time to run before expiry the present value of the exercise price will be reduced and this present value will be dependent on the level of interest rates and the length of time to expiry. In addition, with time to expiry there is a chance that the share price will rise prior to expiry date. The greater the volatility of the share the greater will be the chance of a higher value and thus a higher value of the option at expiry date. It should be noted that although greater volatility implies a higher downside as well as upside value, it is only the upside value that is of interest to us in option valuation. As noted earlier, options cannot have negative value and therefore whether the current price of the stock is 5p or £5 below the exercise price at expiry date the option value will be the same — zero.

Shown in Fig. 10.1 is the theoretical value line compared with the actual value line of a call option. Provided there is some time to run before expiry the actual value line will always plot above the theoretical value line.

A typical option contract requires the option buyer to pay a premium to the option writer who is agreeing either to buy or sell securities for a specified sum at a specified future date. The gain or loss made by the buyer of the option is exactly mirrored in the opposite direction by that

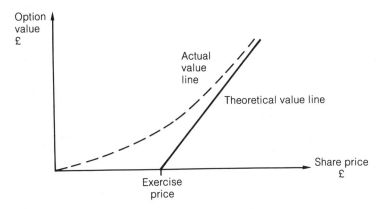

Fig. 10.1.   Relation between option price and share price.

of the writer of the option. For this reason the whole of the option deal is sometimes referred to as a 'zero sum game'. This is an important point and should be borne in mind when appraising options of any kind — the holder of the option can only gain at the expense of the writer.

If options are a zero sum game, why should they be of interest to investors who are not pure speculators and to corporate management? The answer is that in certain circumstances they can reduce overall risk by hedging and may also be a way of changing the pattern of payments to or from the company.

Examples of options are as follows:

1.   An investment manager knows he will receive funds in six months' time which he would like to invest in a security which he believes to be currently attractively valued. To safeguard himself against a substantial increase in value, the manager could purchase a six month call option enabling him to buy the security at its current market value. The premium he would be required to pay would depend upon the five factors outlined earlier.
2.   Any underwriting agreement can be viewed as a put option. Here a fee is paid to the underwriter which can be viewed as the option premium in return for which the underwriter agrees to take up any shares not taken up in the issue.

These are but two examples among many which could be cited.

Convertibles
Convertibles are debentures or loan stock which carry the right to convert into ordinary shares at a specified price at or between certain dates. The coupon rate of the convertible is typically lower than debt of similar risk and it is sometimes regarded as cheaper because of this. However, the question of comparative cost will depend on the conversion price and terms. A convertible can be viewed as debt plus an option. The debt part can be valued by reference to debt of a similar risk, maturity and coupon rate. The option value can be related to the five factors previously

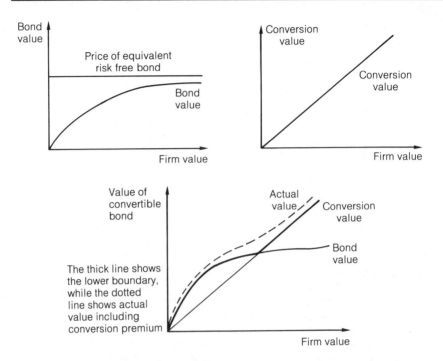

Fig. 10.2.   Determinants of convertible values.

discussed which affect option value, viz. variability of stock price, risk-free interest rate, time to exercise date, exercise price and current share price.

The price of a convertible depends therefore on its **bond value** and its **conversion value**. The bond value is what the bond would sell for if it could not be converted. The conversion value is what the bond would sell for if it had to be converted immediately.

There are therefore two lower bounds to the price of any convertible: its bond value and its conversion value. The bond value will tend to vary with the fortunes of the firm. If the firm is doing very well then the bond value will approach that of the price of an equivalent risk-free bond. However, if the firm is doing badly, investors will demand a higher rate of return on the bond, thus forcing the bond price down. Bond value will usually exceed conversion value when the firm is doing comparatively poorly and firm value is low. If the firm is doing well then conversion value will take over as the principal determinant of convertible value. Figure 10.2 illustrates these factors affecting convertible values.

Advantages of convertibles to company:

1.   Lower coupon rate than equivalent debt conserving cash flow.
2.   Interest paid is tax deductible.
3.   Debt self-liquidating on conversion into shares.
4.   May be seen as a way of issuing shares at higher than current market value (but see below).
5.   Gearing ratio improved when conversion takes place.

Advantages of convertibles to investor:

1. Dual support to price through bond and conversion values.
2. Lower taxable income than equivalent debt but with likelihood of capital gain on conversion.
3. Security of debt with potential conversion giving 'share of the action'.
4. May be seen as a cheap way of acquiring equity (but see below).

It will be noted in the above lists of advantages that both the company and shareholders sometimes claim they are either issuing shares at a premium or acquiring at a potential discount! It was pointed out in the discussion on options that the buyer of the option could only gain at the expense of the writer or vice versa. Exactly the same applies in appraising the conversion value of convertibles. If the initial price of the convertibles is correctly and fairly fixed then both company and investor will get a fair deal.

In recent years companies have issued convertibles which in addition to carrying conversion rights into equity also allow holders to demand repayment at a previously agreed premium over issue price. These issues are sometimes referred to as 'puttable convertibles'; that is the holder has a dual option, a call on equity and a put on the bond. On issue the assumption has been that conversion will take place. The issues have often been made to finance expansion and acquisitions in times of buoyant stock market prices. However, when prices fell, companies found themselves with larger liabilities than anticipated and this has led to a number of problems where companies are experiencing difficulty in funding both interest and repayment. Reported profits are also affected by the need to charge extra interest implied in the higher repayment value and liabilities also need to be increased to reflect the likelihood of repayment rather than conversion.

Warrants

Warrants are essentially long-term call options giving the holder the right to purchase shares in the company at a stated exercise price on or between certain future dates. Warrants are sometimes issued attached to debt but they are usually detachable, meaning that they may be exercised apart from the security with which they were offered. Warrant holders are not entitled to vote, nor do they receive cash dividends. Their interest in the company is usually protected against future changes in the capital structure. The exercise price is often increased over the life of the warrant. Although the Black–Scholes option valuation formula may be used to value a warrant, dividend payments and potential dilution arising from the additional shares potentially outstanding present difficulties.

Warrants are often attached to loan stocks to give a 'sweetener' to financing packages. This is particularly so in the case of smaller companies where lenders are thus enabled to share in potential growth of the company without investing equity money from the outset. As with convertibles, advantages are suggested for warrants which a student of market efficiency should at least doubt. It is sometimes suggested that warrants are a way of agreeing to sell equity at a price higher than the existing market price, this from the company's point of view.

Alternatively, holders of warrants might be encouraged to believe that it is potentially a cheap way into the company's equity. As warrants are long-term options and we saw that from the point of view of holder and writer options are a zero sum game, these arguments can be quickly disposed of.

Valuation of options

The most sophisticated option valuation model devised to date is the Black–Scholes formula. In addition to its use in valuing traded options, adaptations have also been made to help value convertibles and warrants. The formula is as follows:

$$\text{Present value of call option} = PN(d_1) - EXe^{-r_f t}N(d_2)$$

where

$$d_1 = \frac{\log{(P/EX)} + r_f t + \sigma^2 t/2}{\sigma\sqrt{t}}$$

$$d_2 = \frac{\log{(P/EX)} + r_f t - \sigma^2 t/2}{\sigma\sqrt{t}}$$

$N(d)$ = cumulative normal probability density function
EX = exercise price of option
t = time to exercise date
P = price of stock now
σ^2 = variance per period of (continuously compounded) rate of return on the stock
r_f = (continuously compounded) risk-free rate of interest

The formula says that an options value increases with the level of the stock price relative to the exercise price (P/EX), the time to expiration times the interest rate ($r_f t$), and the time to expiration times the stocks' variability ($\sigma^2 t$).

We will illustrate aspects of convertibles and warrants using a question taken from the Certified Accountants examinations of December 1987.

Example
Several years ago Nopen PLC issued 15%, 15 year loan stock with warrants attached. The warrants may be exercised at any time during the next four years and each warrant allows the purchase of one ordinary share at a price of 400p. The company has also issued a 9% convertible debenture which is due for redemption at the par value of £100 in five years' time. Conversion rights, which are available at any time up to the redemption date, allow the conversion of one debenture into 25 ordinary shares. The current market yield on straight debentures for a company of Nopen's risk class is 12% per year.

Estimate the minimum market price of a warrant and of a £100 convertible debenture if the current share price of Nopen is 300p, 420p and 500p.

Explain why the market price of a warrant or convertible debenture is likely to be more than the price that you have estimated.

Taxation may be ignored.

Solution and discussion
The warrants can be exercised at any time over the next four years. We need to compare the current market value of the shares with the purchase/exercise price.

Current share price possibilities	300p	420p	500p
Exercise price	400p	400p	400p
	(100p)	20p	100p

As warrants (like other options) do not have negative values the minimum market price given a share value of 300p would be zero. With values of 420p and 500p, minimum warrant values would be as shown, 20p and 100p respectively. The minimum value of the convertible will be the higher of bond value or conversion value.

Conversion value

Current share price possibilities	300p	420p	500p
Conversion values ($\times 25$)	£75	£105	£125

Bond values
There will be one bond value equal to the present value of the cash flows to be derived from ownership if the bond is not converted

$$\text{Bond value} = \sum_{t=1}^{5} \frac{9}{(1 + 0.12)^t} + \frac{100}{(1 + 0.12)^5}$$

= £89.18 (if interest is paid half-yearly value will be £89)

With a current share price of 300p the minimum value of the convertible will be £89, the bond value. However, with values of 420p and 500p the minimum value will be the conversion values of £105 and £125 respectively.

As long as the option element of each security has time to run before expiry it is likely that the market price will be above the minimum values calculated. This is because there is a probability of the market value of the share increasing prior to expiry, leading to a higher value on expiry.

11 Capital structure policy

Introduction

Gearing, or **leverage** as it is also called, refers to the existence of debt in the capital structure of a company.

Debt holders face less risk than equity shareholders as they receive a fixed interest return irrespective of whether profits are earned and are entitled to repayment of their loans in priority to shareholders. The return on debt is therefore lower than that on equity. If profits are rising the existence of debt can lead to a higher rate of growth in earnings per share but with declining profits the equity shareholders become more vulnerable. The existence of debt in the capital structure adds to the risk faced by equity shareholders as the volatility of their returns increases. This is illustrated below.

Illustration 1

Companies with different levels of gearing (000s)

	A	B	C
Equity — shares of £1	100 000	80 000	50 000
12% debt	—	20 000	50 000
	£100 000	£100 000	£100 000

Effect on EPS of different levels of profit/gearing (000s)

	A			B			C		
Profits	8 000	12 000	20 000	8 000	12 000	20 000	8 000	12 000	20 000
Interest	—	—	—	2 400	2 400	2 400	6 000	6 000	6 000
	8 000	12 000	20 000	5 600	9 600	17 600	2 000	6 000	14 000
Taxation	2 800	4 200	7 000	1 960	3 360	6 160	700	2 100	4 900
(35%)	5 200	7 800	13 000	3 640	6 240	11 440	1 300	3 900	9 100
EPS	5.2p	7.8p	13p	4.55p	7.8p	14.3p	2.6p	7.8p	18.2p

If company earns 12% on total capital to give profits of £12 000 the EPS is the same irrespective of level of gearing. If company earnings are above

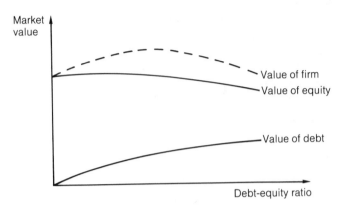

Fig. 11.1. Traditional view of debt and value of firm.

12% then EPS increases as gearing rises, but if rate of earnings is less than 12% then EPS decreases with higher gearing.

As debt carries a lower rate of return, does it lead to a lower overall cost of capital? This question has been the subject of debate for a considerable number of years.

Traditional theory

The traditional theory of gearing and cost of capital supported the view that it was possible to reduce cost of capital and increase the value of the firm by taking on gearing to some optimum level. This view is illustrated in Fig. 11.1.

It was held by traditionalists that at low levels of gearing, equity holders would not require a large premium to compensate for the financial risk faced, but this attitude would change as the level became greater and in addition debtholders would require higher returns as gearing increased. Thus there would be an optimum level of debt at which cost of capital would be minimized and value of the firm maximized. This seems to suggest that shareholders are rather slow to recognize the risk debt brings to the capital structure.

Arbitrage

Modigliani and Miller (MM) showed that under a restrictive set of assumptions, gearing would have no effect on either cost of capital or firm value. They assumed perfect markets with no taxes or transaction costs; in addition they assumed the existence of firms of the same business risk and that personal borrowing was a perfect substitute for corporate borrowing. With such assumptions they showed that it was the income generated by the firm which determined value rather than the way this income was split between providers of capital. If two firms with the same

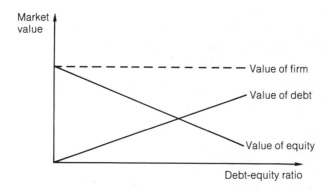

Fig. 11.2. MM(no taxation) and value of firm.

level of business risk but different levels of gearing sold for different values, then shareholders would move from the overvalued to under-valued firm and adjust their level of borrowing through the market to maintain financial risk at the same level. In this way shareholders would increase their income while maintaining their investment and risk at the same level. This process of **arbitrage** would drive the price of the two firms to a common process of equilibrium total value. MM's view is illustrated in Fig. 11.2.

An important implication of MM is that WACC is a constant. This is because the return required on equity rises to exactly offset the lower cost of debt taken on.

Although this sometimes seems an extreme view to advance, consider the case of an investor who owns all the equity of a company. Is it suggested that he could increase his wealth/value of firm by trading in equity for an issue of debt?!

MM's original view led to the espousal of three propositions as follows.

Proposition 1
The market value of a firm is independent of its capital structure and is given by capitalizing its total earnings at the capitalization rate appropriate to an all-equity company of that risk class.

Proposition 2
The expected rate of return on equity increases linearly with the gearing ratio as follows:

$$R_E = R_U + \frac{V_D}{V_E}(R_U - R_D)$$

R_E = cost of equity, R_U = cost of equity for all equity firm, R_D = cost of debt, V_D = market value of debt, V_E = market value of equity.

As cost of equity increases as debt is added to the capital structure the weighted-average cost of capital is the same irrespective of the level of gearing.

Proposition 3

The hurdle rate in project appraisal is the rate of return appropriate to an all-equity firm. This follows from Proposition 2 which ensures that the weighted average cost of capital is constant.

Illustration 2. MM arbitrage

	Lilley	*Thompson*
Equity	5 000 000	4 000 000
10% debt	—	2 000 000
	5 000 000	6 000 000
Profit before interest	1 000 000	1 000 000

Chappell owns 5% of Thompson's equity. His income will be

$$\begin{array}{lr} \text{Total Thompson profit} & 1\,000\,000 \\ \text{Less: debt interest} & \underline{200\,000} \\ & £800\,000 \\ \times \dfrac{5}{100} = £ & \underline{40\,000} \end{array}$$

MM would say that Lilley and Thompson should both have the same total value because they have identical cash flows and risk level. Chappell should therefore sell his equity in Thompson for £200 000 (5% of £4M), borrow £100 000 at 10% to maintain his own level of risk (both business and personal) and invest £300 000 in Lilley's equity. He will then own 6% of Lilley. Chappell's income will then be:

$$\begin{array}{lr} \text{Total Lilley income} & £1\,000\,000 \\ \times \dfrac{6}{100} = & 60\,000 \\ \text{Less: interest on loan} & \underline{10\,000} \\ 10\% \times 100\,000 & \\ & £ \quad \underline{50\,000} \end{array}$$

Chappell has therefore increased his income by £10 000 while maintaining his total risk at the same level. MM said that this arbitrage activity would result in the values of Lilley and Thompson moving to the same equilibrium value. Note the dependency on assumption of perfect markets and equivalent risk classes.

MM agreed that with corporate taxes borrowing would increase the value of the firm because of the value of the tax shield on interest paid.

Firms value = Value if all equity
            + PV of tax shield, assuming perpetual debt,

$$\text{PV of tax shield} = tV_D$$

where t = rate of corporation tax and V_D = value of debt in issue.
    Likewise cost of capital would be reduced to

$$\frac{R_U(1 - V_D t)}{V_0}$$

where V_0 = total value of debt and equity ($V_D + V_E$).

MM with corporate taxes seems to suggest that 99.9% debt would be optimum as value is theoretically increased as more debt is taken on. However, as the level of debt increases lenders are likely to demand higher rates of interest and might also place an upper limit on the gearing ratio the company can operate at. Bankruptcy costs both direct and indirect must also be considered as an inhibiting factor on higher levels of gearing.

Analysis of Miller

Miller (1977) suggested that there was a need to consider personal as well as corporate taxes in evaluating gearing. His analysis assumed that no personal tax was paid on equity (all benefits received in form of capital gains) but debt interest suffered tax at the shareholder's marginal rate. Initially some shareholders (e.g. pension funds) would be prepared to take on debt as they are nil taxpayers. However, as more debt was issued to shareholders paying tax at low marginal rates higher interest would have to be offered to compensate for the tax shareholders would pay on the interest. Eventually a point would be reached where the corporate tax saved by the company would equal the personal tax (and hence extra interest) paid by the holder. At this point issue of debt would cease. Miller suggested that this would lead to an optimum macro level of debt for the corporate sector as a whole. Miller's theory is illustrated in Fig. 11.3.

Care must be exercised in translating this model to the UK because of the different tax systems.

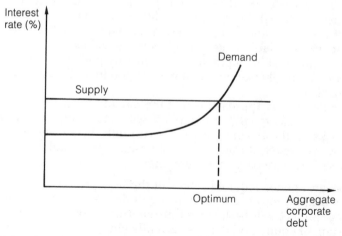

Fig. 11.3. Aggregrate supply and demand for corporate debt.

Practical issues in levels of debt

In the preceding discussion, various views on the significance of debt in the capital structure have been examined.

There is general agreement that debt can add value of the company if only because of the tax deductibility of debt interest. However, this is only the case if there are taxable profits to offset the interest against. Along with increasing risk and potential bankruptcy the possibility of 'tax exhaustion' should also keep debt levels within reasonable limits. A further factor is that as more and more debt is added to the capital structure so company management may find more conditions being imposed on their courses of action through the imposition of debt covenants; additionally management may wish to retain flexibility by retaining unused but usable sources of further borrowing.

The type of business may also affect the level of gearing of individual companies. Those with tangible marketable assets, e.g. property, will usually be able to borrow more. Lenders will see greater security and there will be lower expected bankruptcy costs in administering this type of asset. On the other hand, firms with assets consisting mainly of intangible unmarketable assets may find, and perhaps should find, lenders less willing to advance loans which lead to a high level of gearing.

Weighted average cost of capital (WACC)

Prior to the development of the capital asset pricing model, cost of capital for project appraisal was usually related to a company cost of capital figure. This cost of capital is obtained by first computing the individual costs of equity, debt and any other capital employed. These costs are then combined into a single cost of capital figure by weighting each of the individual costs by the proportion each represents in the value of the company. The weighting should be on the basis of current market value (as we shall see costs are determined on the basis of current market values and expectations), but because of difficulties sometimes associated with market values, balance sheet values are sometimes used. It is difficult to justify the use of balance sheet values as these will usually be based on historic values and will be dependent on company policy on such matters as revaluation of tangible assets, treatment of goodwill, brand names and other intangibles.

The rationale for this approach is that the rate of return currently being demanded by investors in the company will reflect their view of the perceived risks of the business activities currently being undertaken by the company. However, if this rate is to be used as the required return for a new project it is necessary to assume that

1. The risk and hence required return of the new project is equal to the average of the projects currently being undertaken by the company.
2. The new project will be financed in the same way — with the same proportion of equity and debt as currently employed by the company.
3. If there is debt in the capital structure and relief is obtained on debt

interest paid, then use of WACC assumes both perpetual debt and a permanent tax shield at current tax rates.

Cost of equity

Equity shares carry no right to a fixed return but holders are entitled to the residue of profits after contractual obligations to other providers of capital are met. Equity shareholders are perpetual investors and shares are normally purchased in the expectation that dividends will be paid and that these dividends will grow over time. The value of an ordinary share can be expressed as the sum of the present value of all future dividends to be recovered. If V_E is the current value of a share, D_t the dividend to be received in period t and $100R_E\%$ the return required for investing in equity (the cost of equity), then

$$V_E = \sum_{t=1}^{N} \frac{D_t}{(1 + R_E)^t}$$

If it is assumed that dividends will grow at $100g\%$ per annum in perpetuity then the current value can be represented by the Gordon growth model, named after its popularizer,

$$V_E = \frac{D_1}{R_E - g}$$

In the equation D_1 refers to the dividend payment one period from now and can be expressed in terms of the dividend just paid as $D_0(1 + g)$.

If we arrange the Gordon growth model we obtain an equation for the cost of equity as follows,

$$R_E = \frac{D_1}{V_E} + g$$

We can see that the return/cost of equity is a combination of dividend yield and expected growth.

Bearing in mind that $D_1 = D_0 (1 + g)$ and that the current value of the share can be obtained from the market the crucial figure for estimating the cost of equity is the growth figure. Estimates of growth can be obtained in at least two ways. Firstly average growth of dividends, or earnings if more appropriate, can be computed for a number of years up to the present time and an assumption made about future long-term growth based on this historic average growth figure. Care needs to be taken in merely extrapolating historic growth into the future; there is evidence which suggests that growth does not necessarily follow a constant pattern. The second way in which a growth figure can be estimated is by using the average proportion of earnings retained each year and multiplying this by the average rate of return the company earns on its assets.

Example

Holly plc has just paid a dividend of 10p per share on its ordinary shares which are currently quoted at 220p ex dividend. In recent years, dividends and earnings have grown by an average of 10% each year while the company, again on average, has retained 50% of its earnings. The company earns a return of 20% per annum on assets used in the business. What is the cost of equity capital?

Solution
An average growth rate of dividends and earnings of 10% is given. In fact this is the same as retentions multiplied by return on assets, $0.5 \times 0.2 = 0.1$, 10%; this equality will not always be the case.

If we then plug the values given into the cost of equity capital we get

$$R_E = \frac{10(1 + 0.1)}{220} + 0.1$$
$$= 0.15 \ (15\%)$$

The cost of equity is thus 15%. Note that the market value used is the current ex dividend market value.

Cost of debt
The cost of debt can be obtained in a similar way to that used for equity, the objective being to determine the current market rate of interest investors require for investing in the company debt.

With debt the payments to investors will normally be set out at issue and will be fixed both in terms of interest and amounts payable on redemption (repayment on maturity). This need not necessarily be the case as redemption values could, for example, be index linked to the retail price index. However index linking is not very popular with private-sector companies and it is more often the case that fixed-interest returns are just as their name suggests, fixed.

Fixed-interest securities can be irredeemable with no repayment date fixed, or as is the usual case, with a specified date or dates set for redemption. If debt is perpetual then the value, V_D, of £100 nominal value of stock can be expressed as

$$V_D = \frac{I}{R_D}$$

where I is the annual interest payment per £100 of stock and R_D is the return required by investors. Values are related to £100 of stock as this is the normal dealing unit.

The equation can be rearranged to express the cost of debt as follows,

$$R_D = \frac{I}{V_D}$$

It is more usual for debt to be redeemable and in this case the valuation formula becomes

$$V_D = \sum_{t=1}^{N} \frac{I}{(1 + R_D)^t} + \frac{M}{(1 + R_D)^N}$$

Where M is the amount due on redemption per £100 of stock; if redemption is at par then $M = £100$.

The equation is in the form of an IRR (Chapter 2) which must be solved to obtain the cost of debt R_D.

Example

Holly plc has only one issue of debt outstanding. The debt has a 9% coupon (i.e. pays £9 per £100 of stock issued) which is paid annually and is due to be repaid at par in five years' time. If the stock is currently quoted at £89 what is the cost of debt? Using the valuation formula above,

$$89 = \sum_{t=1}^{5} \frac{9}{(1 + R_D)^t} + \frac{100}{(1 + R_D)^5}$$

The equation can be solved for R_D by trial and error or by using a calculator. Using a calculator gives a rate of 12% (rounded from 12.06%). Having calculated the cost of both equity and debt the weighted average cost of capital can be calculated.

Example

Holly plc has 10 million shares with a nominal value of £1 in issue with a current market value of 220p per share ex dividend and £5 million 9% debt with a current market value of £89 per £100 of stock. In this calculation market values should be used.

$$\text{WACC} = \frac{(10 \times 2.2)\,(0.15)}{(10 \times 2.2) + (5 \times 0.89)} + \frac{(5 \times 0.89)\,(0.12)}{(10 \times 2.2) + (5 \times 0.89)}$$
$$= 0.1449\ (14.5\%)$$

If MV_E and MV_D represent total market value of equity and debt respectively then,

$$\text{WACC} = \frac{MV_E \times R_E}{MV_E + MV_D} + \frac{MV_D \times R_D}{MV_E + MV_D}$$
$$= \frac{(MV_E \times R_E) + (MV_D + R_D)}{MV_E + MV_D}$$

With corporation tax and the tax deductibility of debt interest the cost of debt is reduced to $R_D(1 - t)$ where 100t% is the rate of corporation tax. In our example with a tax rate of 35% this reduces the cost of debt to $12(1 - 0.35) = 7.8\%$ and WACC is reduced to 13.8% with 7.8% substituted for 12% in the calculations.

We now have two ways to calculate a cost of capital. One method, the CAPM project-based approach, uses a cost of capital relative to the project and ignores financing. WACC considers both project risk and financing implications. Use of WACC assumes the following:

1. The project being appraised is of the same risk as the average of projects currently being undertaken.
2. The project will be financed by the same level of gearing currently used by the company.
3. Debt is perpetual and offers a perpetual cash shield benefit.
4. All investment projects are perpetuities.

Adjusted present value (APV)

Use of WACC requires assumptions listed above. However, different projects may be capable of supporting different levels of debt and the debt capacity of any project may vary over the life of the project particularly as the project declines in value.

If CAPM and an ungeared project beta is used in the evaluation then explicit adjustment will have to be made for financing or any other side effects. Supporters of APV advocate that this approach is superior.

The present value of the project is first determined assuming that it is an all equity-financed mini-firm. This is referred to as the base case net present value. The present value of any side effects are then calculated and added or subtracted from the base case NPV. Examples of side effects would be tax shield on loan interest payments, subsidized loans, issue costs, etc.:

$$\text{APV} = \text{Base case NPV} \pm \text{PV of side effects}$$

The PV of side effects should be calculated using the discount rate appropriate to the cash flows under appraisal.

In fact given a project which satisfies the assumptions for the use of WACC then either WACC, MM's adjusted discount rate or the APV approach would give the same result.

Example
Barry plc has a capital structure comprising 60% equity and 40% debt. It is appraising a project requiring the investment of £10000 to yield £1536 in perpetuity commencing one year after investment. The beta of the company's equity β_E has been calculated to be 1.4 and it pays 12% interest on debt R_D which is also the risk-free rate R_f. The current rate of corporation tax t is 35% and the expected market return R_M is 18%.

You are required to appraise the project and illustrate the equivalence of APV, WACC and MM's adjusted discount rate under the conditions stated.

WACC
Using CAPM to calculate the required return on equity we have

$$R_E = R_f + \beta_E(R_m - R_f)$$
$$= 0.12 + 1.4(0.18 - 0.12)$$
$$= 0.204 \ (20.4\%)$$

$$\text{WACC} = \frac{(0.6) \ (0.204) + (0.4) \ (0.12) \ (1 - 0.35)}{0.6 + 0.4}$$

$$= 0.1536 \ (15.36\%)$$

$$\text{NPV of project} = -10\,000 + \frac{1536}{0.1536}$$

$$= 0$$

After taking financing into account NPV of project is zero.

APV

Ungear equity beta to obtain return required on project (i.e. as if company was financed entirely by equity):

$$\beta_p = \frac{\beta_E}{1 + (D/E)\,(1 - t)}$$

$$= \frac{1.4}{1 + (0.4/0.6)\,(1 - 0.35)}$$

$$= \underline{0.9767}$$

$$R_u = 0.12 + 0.9767(0.18 - 0.12)$$
$$= 0.1786\ (17.86\%)$$

Using APV, the APV of project is calculated by discounting the cash flows at the project rate, i.e. the rate if all equity financed, and then adding in any financing side effects. In this case this will be the perpetually capitalized value of the tax shield on the debt interest payable. The project is valued at £10 000 and with 40% debt finance will require £4000 debt.

$$\text{Annual interest} = 4000 \times 0.12$$
$$= 480$$

$$\text{Annual tax shield} = 480 \times 0.35$$
$$= 168$$

$$\text{APV} = -1000 + \frac{1536}{0.1786} + \frac{168}{0.12}$$
$$= -1000 + 8600 + 1400$$
$$= 0$$

APV and WACC thus give the same result. Note that the tax shield benefit is capitalized using the before tax interest rate. This is the appropriate rate for these cash flows as the tax shield is considered certain. The pre-tax rate must be used to avoid double counting of the tax benefit.

MM adjusted discount rate

The adjusted rate is obtained using the all equity rate computed in the APV section.

$$\text{Adjusted rate} = R_u\left(1 - \frac{V_D}{V_E + V_D}\,t\right)$$

$$= 0.1786\left(1 - \frac{0.4}{0.4 + 0.6}\,0.35\right)$$

$$= 0.1536\ (15.36\%)$$

This is the same as the WACC rate. Like WACC it incorporates the financing side effects and would be used in the same way.

We can thus see that under the conditions assumed, all three approaches give the same result. To obtain this similarity it was necessary to assume

1. Project had same risk as those currently being undertaken.
2. Project and debt are perpetual.
3. Gearing level remains the same.

In smaller projects, violations of these assumptions may not cause material differences in the calculation of project NPVs. However, larger projects, those with special financing deals and those with different levels of risk might be better appraised using APV. This would enable project specific risk-adjusted returns to be used and any side effects could be separately identified and valued for appraisal purposes.

12   Dividend policy

Introduction

This chapter deals with the payment of dividends to ordinary shareholders. Unlike preference shares and other forms of capital, ordinary shares carry no specific dividend rights. The payment of ordinary dividends is a matter of company policy and depends upon such factors as the existence of distributable profits, liquidity of company and the existence of profitable investment opportunities.

The proportion of profits paid out as dividends can vary considerably from company to company. At first sight it might appear that the highest dividend possible would be best for shareholders, particularly as valuation models of equity are often based on the present value of future dividends. However, it is the pattern of dividends over time which creates the highest present value which maximizes shareholder wealth; if the payment of a high dividend in the current year means that investment must be forgone in a profitable project, then a low or even zero dividend might be preferable. This point is illustrated later in the chapter. Other factors which could affect dividend payments are taxation, both personal and corporate, and the use of dividends as providers of information in uncertain conditions.

Over the years there has been a certain amount of controversy on the value of dividend payments to shareholders. Initially there was a reasonable degree of acceptance that high dividends increased shareholder wealth and although there are those that still hold this view, other persuasive arguments have been advanced. Miller and Modigliani (MM) suggested that dividends were neutral and irrelevant to the value of shares while another school of thought advanced the view that dividends reduced shareholder wealth because dividend income was taxed more highly than equivalent capital gains. We will discuss these views in the context of current market conditions and tax legislation.

Do dividend payments increase shareholder wealth?

The original view of dividends was that investors would apply a lower discount rate to dividends to be received in the near future than to more distant capital gains. The argument was that payment of dividends resolved uncertainty and is often referred to as the 'bird-in-hand' argument.

Market analysts also supported this view and high dividend payers were capitalized more highly than low payers. However, it is not enough to consider dividend payments in isolation; the effect of payments on investment strategies must be considered. Many companies highly rated by the stock market pay very low or, in some cases, no dividend at all. Why should this be? The answer is simple enough; these companies are often regarded as being in a high-growth situation and may include smaller companies which are expanding from a relatively small capital base. Investors are prepared to forgo current dividends in the expectation that rapid growth will lead to much higher profits, out of which substantial dividend payments may eventually be paid. This seems to suggest that perhaps dividends may not be as important as was first suggested, a view supported by MM.

Irrelevancy of dividend payments (MM)

MM viewed dividends as neutral (irrelevant). They assumed a world of perfect capital markets and perfect certainty where all market participants were aware of the future investment programme and profits of all companies. In these circumstances, companies could be correctly valued on the basis of their future cash flows and these values reflected in share price. If shareholders had different consumption requirements in any year they could adjust their cash preferences by either selling or buying shares through the perfect market assumed where there would be no taxes or transaction costs. Any cash dividend payments made by companies would lead to a reduction in share price equal to the dividend payment made reflecting the outflow of resources from the company to shareholders.

Illustration of MM view on dividend policy

1. We assume an all equity company with 10 million shares in issue, each having a current market value of 840p per share. The company is currently valued at £84 million which reflects the present value of its business activities. It is further assumed that the company's cash resources are committed to investment in business activities and it has no spare cash resources to pay a dividend.
2. The company has always paid a dividend and the directors wish to maintain this record by paying a dividend of 40p per share which will require cash of 10M × 40p = £4M.
3. If the company is to maintain its investment programme then the £4M required to pay the dividend will have to be obtained by issuing new shares to outside investors.
4. After payment of the dividend the company and individual share value will be

	Company	*Share*
Before dividend	£84 000 000	840p
Cash dividend	4 000 000	40p
After dividend	80 000 000	800p

5. The company will have to issue shares to the value of £4M and will issue

$$\frac{4\,000\,000}{8} = 500\,000 \text{ shares}$$

The issue of 500 000 shares at 800p will bring in £4M cash thus replacing the cash used to pay dividend to the 'old shareholders'. The latter will have received dividend of 40p per share and have a share now valued at 800p; before payment of the dividend they hold shares valued at 840p. There has thus been no change in the wealth of the original shareholders, only in the form it takes.

6. Why could the new shares not be sold at the old price of 840p? Because markets are assumed to be perfect and therefore investors will know that the dividend payment is being made to existing shareholders, thus reducing the assets of the company and the value of the equity.

		Shareholders	
Company assets		*Before dividend*	*After dividend*
£84M		10M shares	Old shareholders
		at 840p	10M shares at
		= £84M	(840−40)p
			= £80M

New shareholders
0.5M shares at
800p
= £4M

Dividend of £4M cash
paid and replaced
with new issue proceeds
of same amount

This emphasizes that share value is determined by company value which itself is determined by the present value of its future business activities. To emphasize this point consider the following example.

Example
An all equity company has in issue five million shares with a current market value of £12 per share valuing the company at £60M. The company has £5M in cash which can either be used to pay a dividend of £1 per share or invested in a project which has an NPV of £5M. Should the company pay the dividend or invest in the project?

Solution
If the company pays a dividend then total value falls by £5M to £55M. Shareholders will receive a dividend of £1 per share and will hold shares valued at £11 each (55M/5M). Their total wealth will remain unchanged at £12 per share originally held.

On the other hand, if the company does not pay a dividend but invests instead in the new project the value of the company increases by the NPV of the project to £65M (£60M + NPV of £5M). Shareholders' wealth will be increased by this strategy as they will now hold shares valued at £13 each (£65M/5M).

This example once again relies on the existence of perfect markets where participants will know of the new investment and its value to the company.

Early criticism of MM questioned why it was that if dividend payments were irrelevant, share prices tended to rise when dividends increased and to decline when dividends were reduced. MM responded by saying that it was not the actual dividend changes which caused the price change but the information conveyed by the changes. Increases were viewed as good news and a sign of optimism about the future, while decreases would give the opposite impression. The information role of dividends has been the subject of many articles in the finance literature. MM also rationalized the existence of both high and low payout dividend companies by postulating a 'clientele effect'. Different investors would prefer different levels of dividend payments. Younger investors with good salaries might be prepared to forgo high current dividend payments and receive their increases in wealth in the form of capital gains; dividends for consumption purposes would not be a pressing need for them. On the other hand, there would be a group of older, perhaps retired, investors who would need dividends for consumption purposes. The existence of transaction costs in real markets would lead to investors choosing companies with a dividend policy matching their consumption requirements and there would be 'clienteles' for companies with varying payout policies.

Taxation and dividend payments

Personal and company taxation may both have implications for dividend payouts; we first consider personal taxation. In most tax regimes, dividend payments are taxed at the shareholder's marginal rate of income tax. This led to the proposal in the USA that it might be better for shareholders to have no dividend but to receive their benefits in the form of capital gains, which at the time of the proposal were subject to a lower rate of tax. It was pointed out that for companies to pay dividends subject to personal tax and then make rights issues would lead to shareholder losses through tax payments and the transaction costs of new issues. This was particularly so in the USA where there is a classical tax system (see Chapter 1), but less so in the UK where, with an imputation system, tax exempt investors (e.g. pension funds) can reclaim imputed tax. In fact, both in the UK and USA, capital gains are now taxed on the same basis as dividends, at the shareholders' marginal tax rate. Capital gains still have advantages; they are charged only on realization and there is an annual exemption limit for individuals of, currently, £5 500.

In recent years, companies have substantially increased dividend payments and investors, particularly the institutions, have become accustomed to regular increases. As mentioned above pension funds find dividends particularly attractive because of their tax position. The existence of shareholders with different marginal rates of tax has led to the suggestion that there might be a clientele effect with exempt shareholders favouring companies with high payout policies while low payout companies might be preferred by high rate taxpayers.

There could also be a tax deterrent for some companies to pay high levels of dividends. Whenever a company pays a dividend Advanced Corporation Tax (ACT) has to be paid to the inland revenue. Although the ACT can subsequently be offset against mainstream tax liability, this can only be done if sufficient taxable profits are available. Companies which might find themselves in difficulties include those with high tax allowances, e.g. capital allowances; those with available tax losses; companies with substantial overseas income where double taxation relief is given in the UK, thus reducing UK taxable income.

Dividend payments in practice

We will now seek to reconcile the alternative views briefly examined in the previous sections. Despite the extreme views advanced on dividend policy, research and behaviour seem to indicate that market participants consider dividends to be important. Research indicates that company managers consider dividend policy a prime decision factor. Managers seek to smooth dividend payments from year to year; significant changes in profits are not immediately reflected as dividends. Large profit increases lead to a graduated increase in dividends, while when profits fall, managers may well seek to maintain current dividend levels. Indeed in early 1991 some companies reporting lower profits proposed increases in dividend payments. This behaviour can be attributed to the information content of dividend changes. Managers try and avoid large and unexpected fluctuations because of the potentially adverse information that might be conveyed, leading to uncertainty and a volatile share price. It seems that managers believe that the market will interpret an increase in dividend as conveying optimism about the future level of profits, while a decrease would be interpreted as a pessimistic sign indicating that profits are not expected to increase or perhaps decrease. As managers are very sensitive to factors which they perceive as affecting the share price, it seems that they will be careful not to make changes in dividend payments which will have an adverse effect on their share price.

In addition to the points discussed above there are a number of other factors which could affect dividend payments as follows:

1. Company law requires that dividends be paid out of distributable profits.
2. The company should consider its liquidity position when preparing dividend payments. Is cash available? Has the company loan obligations to fulfil in the near future?
3. Are there debt covenants in existence which limit the ability of the company to maintain or increase its dividend payments?
4. Will the payment of increased dividends limit the company's ability to invest in profitable business projects? Smaller expanding companies with limited access to financial markets may choose to pay

little, or even no, dividend to shareholders. Larger companies may find it easier to raise funds and may not be constrained in this way.

5. We have already referred to tax factors separately but both company and shareholder taxes may impact on dividend policies. Exempt shareholders will prefer dividend payments and as this group represented principally by pension funds becomes more influential, companies may feel obliged to keep increasing their dividends. On the other hand, if companies were currently to have low corporation tax bills, then they might feel constrained to moderate their dividend policy so as not to incur unrelieved ACT and increase, even if only temporarily, their tax liabilities.

Share repurchase

UK company law allows companies to repurchase their own shares. Quoted companies can repurchase shares in three ways:

1. direct purchase in stock market;
2. by arrangement with individual shareholder(s);
3. by tender offer to all shareholders.

Prior permission is required from shareholders and holders of warrants, options or convertibles; clearance is also necessary from the takeover panel. Consideration for repurchased shares must be made from distributable profits and the repurchased shares cancelled.

The tax treatment may be important. The excess of cash paid over capital subscribed is treated as a dividend and ACT must be paid. Where shares are purchased direct from shareholders, repayment of the capital element is treated as such under the capital gains tax rules, while the excess is treated as a net dividend and dealt with accordingly. With a market repurchase all proceeds are treated as capital for tax purposes. Exempt institutions would thus prefer direct repurchase as the tax imputed to the dividend element could be reclaimed.

Reasons suggested for share repurchase include:

1. return of surplus cash to shareholders;
2. way of increasing EPS and perhaps share price (but would the market be fooled?);
3. buy-out of unwelcome large shareholders (greenmail);
4. adjustment of capital structure by reducing equity.

13 Management of working capital

Introduction

Working capital is usually defined as the excess of current assets over current liabilities. It represents the investment of a company's funds in net current assets. The constituent parts of working capital are constantly changing, as is the total amount of working capital employed. This may vary due to seasonal reasons and this factor can be appreciated if we set out a basic equation for working capital including the four main constituent items:

$$\text{Working capital} = \text{Stock} + \text{Debtors} + \text{Cash} - \text{Creditors}$$

The more funds a company has tied up in working capital the less is available for investment in fixed assets, the main revenue-producing assets. It might at first be thought that the objective of the company should be to minimize working capital. We can see that this could be done by minimizing stock, debtors and cash and maximizing creditors. However, this could have dangerous consequences. If stock levels were reduced then raw materials might not be available for production as and when required, leading to breakdown in manufacture. If debtors were pressed for earlier payment they might prefer to buy from other suppliers selling goods but offering longer credit terms. If cash is not available to meet unforeseen liabilities the company might have to obtain loans at short notice, which could prove expensive. If the company tries to extend the time taken to pay creditors it could lead to suppliers refusing to sell further goods to the company or the company's overall credit rating suffering, leading to, amongst other things, a higher cost of borrowing. Therefore working capital management should seek to optimize levels of working capital.

The management of working capital requires at least three questions to be considered:

1. How much should be invested in the different forms of current assets?
2. How should the financing of these current assets be divided between short-term and long-term funds?
3. What percentage of total assets should be in the form of current assets and what percentage in fixed assets?

The management of cash, debtors and stock is dealt with in detail in Chapters 15, 16 and 17 respectively.

Use of accounting ratios

Financial ratios are commonly used by analysts to appraise the profitability, liquidity and efficiency of firms. The idea behind the use of ratios is that although absolute amounts invested in different assets and liabilities may change, the relationship between different groups of assets and liabilities should remain more or less constant, or if changes occur they may provide information to the analyst.

Care must be exercised in the use of accounting ratios, they are more likely to be useful when

1. A time series of the same company is examined for changing trends.
2. The ratios of a single company are compared with some relevant industry average.
3. The time series ratios of a particular company are compared with a similar time series of individual equivalent companies.

Ratios have also acquired significance through their use in bankruptcy prediction models. These models seek to identify common factors existing in the ratios of previously bankrupt companies and incorporate them in a model which will enable successful prediction of bankruptcy to be made. Successful models would obviously be very valuable to bankers, principal creditors and others.

Liquidity ratios relate to the company's ability to meet short-term liabilities and are therefore concerned with current asset and liability items. The following two ratios are used to assess the liquidity position of companies. The first is

$$\text{Current ratio} = \frac{\text{Current assets}}{\text{Current liabilities}} \tag{13.1}$$

Historically the satisfactory norm was taken to be 2:1. However, what is satisfactory can vary with the type of business being considered and can also change over time. In fact current ratios have tended to reduce in recent years which reflects the cost and tightness of money but may also indicate more efficient management of stock and debtors. Hence the point stressed above for comparability over time and with like businesses.

In the second ratio,

$$\text{Quick ratio} = \frac{\text{Quick assets}}{\text{Current liabilities}} \tag{13.2}$$

quick assets are usually taken to be all current assets except for stocks and work in progress, that is all assets which are near to conversion into cash. This ratio can indicate the ability of a business to meet its current liabilities from liquid funds. The 'rule of thumb' norm for this ratio historically was taken to be 1:1. However, in line with the decline in the acceptable level of the current ratio a similar decline has occurred in the quick assets ratio.

Two limitations of these liquidity ratios are that they do not take into account any line of credit the company has available to fund working capital and that they are static giving the position at just one moment in time during the company's trading year. If the current liabilities of the company exceed its liquid assets it would be useful to know how quickly this situation could be put right. The following formula is effectively cash flow based:

$$\frac{\text{Current liabilities} - \text{Quick assets}}{\text{Funds generated by operations in one year}} \times 365 \qquad (13.3)$$

This calculation gives the number of days required to pay off the net current debt where current debt is defined as the difference between current liabilities and quick assets.

Other ratios can be used to determine the efficiency of working capital management. The ratio of working capital turnover is calculated as follows:

$$\frac{\text{Stock} + \text{Debtors} - \text{Creditors}}{\text{Sales}} \qquad (13.4)$$

This ratio considers working capital as a whole but in addition the constituent parts, viz. stock, debtors and creditors could be examined separately to see how well each is being managed.

Bankruptcy models have been developed which incorporate financial ratios to enable company failure to be predicted prior to that failure occurring. The most common statistical tool used has been linear discriminant analysis which takes the form

$$z = ax_1 + bx_2 + cx_3 \text{ etc.}$$

x_1, x_2, x_3 etc. are the variables while a, b, c etc., are weights calculated relating to the variables. Altman in the USA and Taffler in the UK have both produced models of this type. The statistical technique was applied to identify those ratios which best discriminated between companies becoming bankrupt and those not becoming bankrupt. In addition the relative level of importance of discriminating ratios was established and these relate to the weights in the linear equation above. The final 'z score' obtained indicates the likelihood of bankruptcy occurring, a low z score indicating vulnerable companies, a high z score indicating a financially stable company. The ratios used in the models are a mixture of liquidity, profitability and efficiency ratios obtained after numerous computer runs.

The test for any model such as these is how well it can predict future failure. The results seem to be encouraging and has led to the establishment of a commercial organization providing information to bankers and others for a fee.

Operating cycle

Operating cycle is the time between the company's outlay on production expenditure and the inflow of cash from the sale of goods. It is measured in numbers of days and in a manufacturing business would be the sum of the following items:

1. average time raw materials remain in stock less the period of credit taken from suppliers;
2. time taken to produce the goods;
3. number of days inventory of finished goods;
4. average time taken by customers to pay for goods.

It will be useful for management to monitor the operating cycle over time and use it as part of the control process of the business.

The operating cycle only gives a time span in days between production costs and cash returns; it says nothing about the amount of working capital that will be required. If an expansion in production and hence sales is projected and an estimate is required of the increase in working capital likely to be needed, a number of techniques are available.

Additional working capital could be estimated by using the historic relationship between sales and working capital. Ratio (13.4) above could be used for this purpose or each constituent part of working capital calculated separately.

Funds flow statements

Funds flow projections can form part of the planning process. Funds flow statements are perhaps more normally associated with the statements produced as part of the annual financial report. However, projected statements based on a projected future balance sheet can be useful in identifying funding gaps. Potentially the procedure for preparing a projected statement follows similar lines to the preparation of a historic statement. The difference is obvious. In one case, two successive historic balance sheets form the basis; in the other, one historic balance sheet and one projected balance sheet form the basis of preparation.

Funds flow statements are not the same as cash flow statements. Cash budgets which are detailed periodic forecasts of future cash flows will play a key role in planning and are discussed in Chapter 15. Funds flow statements on the other hand show a summary of the sources of funds, e.g. retained profits and issue of shares, for a period of time and how those funds have been deployed (applied) in the business, e.g. in purchase of fixed assets and repayment of loans. Also shown are changes in working capital with increases in current assets and decreases in current liabilities being applications of funds and decreases in current assets and increases in current liabilities.

We will illustrate funds flow statements with an example taken from the Chartered Association of Certified Accountants.

Example
The balance sheets of SAF (1979) Ltd were as shown below. During the year ended 31 March 19–6 the company had

1. sold plant with a written down value of £25 800 for £22 400;
2. made a profit before tax of £749 400 after charging depreciation of the following amounts:

	£
Buildings	4 000
Plant and machinery	110 200
Fixtures and equipment	28 100

SAF (1979) Ltd
Balance sheets as at 31 March

19–5 £	19–5 £		19–6 £	19–6 £
		Fixed assets		
		Tangible assets		
		(at written down		
		values)		
200 000		Land and buildings	196 000	
830 700		Plant and machinery	925 800	
		Fixtures,		
		fittings, tools		
182 400		and equipment	204 600	
	1 213 100			1 326 400
		Investments		
		Investments other		
	10 800	than loans		72 000
		Current assets		
421 500		Stock	381 000	
134 600		Debtors	110 200	
89 200		Bank and cash	92 400	
645 300			583 600	
		Creditors amounts		
		due in less than		
		one year		
		Bank loans and		
—		overdrafts	77 300	
120 900		Trade creditors	9 400	
		Bills of exchange		
16 000		payable	51 900	
		Other creditors		
157 300		Taxation	163 200	
		Proposed		
175 000		dividends	190 500	
469 200			492 300	
	176 100	Net current assets		91 300
		Total assets less		
		current		
	1 400 000	liabilities		1 489 700

	19–5			*19–6*
	Represented by:			
£	£		£	£
		Creditors: amounts due in more than one year		
	400 000	Debenture loans		150 000
		Provisions for liabilities and charges		
		Provision for legal damages		
	56 000	and costs		—
		Capital and Reserves		
		Called-up share		
	700 000	capital		700 000
	5 000	Share premium		5 000
	239 000	Profit and loss		634 700
	1 400 000			1 489 700

Note:
The amounts shown in 19–5 for taxation, proposed dividends and legal damages and costs were paid in year ended 31 March 19–6 at the amounts stated.

Required:
(a) Prepare a Statement of Source and Application of Funds for SAF (1979) Ltd for the year ended 31 March 19–6.
(b) Comment briefly on the financial position of the company disclosed by your answer to (a).

(Chartered Association of Certified Accountants)

Solution
(a)   SAF (1979) Ltd
Statement of Source and Application of Funds for year ended 31 March 19–6
Source of funds

Profit before tax		749 400
Adjustments for items not involving the movement of funds:		
Depreciation (4000 + 110 200 + 28 100)	142 300	
Loss on sale of plant (25 800 − 22 400)	3 400	145 700
Total generated from operations		895 100
Funds from other sources		
Sale of plant		22 400
		917 500

Application of funds

Fixed assets bought: Plant (W1)	231 100	
Fixtures (W2)	50 300	
Investments	61 200	
Tax paid	157 300	
Dividends paid	175 000	
Debentures redeemed	250 000	
Legal damages + costs paid	56 000	980 900
		(63 400)

Decrease in working capital

Decrease in stock	(40 500)	
Decrease in debtors	(24 400)	
Decrease in creditors	111 500	
Decrease in bills of exchange payable	(35 900)	
Movement of net liquid funds:		
Increase in bank and cash	3 200	
Increase in bank overdraft	(77 300)	(63 400)

Workings

(W1)	Plant		
Balance b/fwd	830 700	Sale	25 800
Bought (difference)	231 100	Depreciation	110 200
		Balance c/d	925 800
	1 061 800		1 061 800

(W2)	Fixtures		
Balance b/fwd	182 400	Depreciation	28 100
Bought (difference)	50 300	Balance c/d	204 600
	232 700		232 700

The amount generated from operations consists of profit before tax adjusted for non-cash items, mainly depreciation and any profit or loss on sale of assets. Funds from other sources will comprise the actual amounts received from issue of shares or as in this case sale of fixed assets. It will usually be necessary to summarize the movement on asset accounts as in workings 1 and 2 above. The application of funds shows the amounts actually expended during the year on assets purchased; also shown are the actual payments made for taxation and dividends. The latter are not included in the summary of change in working capital. The change in working capital relates to changes in current assets and liabilities other than taxation and dividends which as stated above are dealt with separately. The net change in working capital then equals the net sources or (as in this example) net application of funds.

(b)   The statement shows that during the year funds generated from operations and other sources did not cover total applications. This was mainly due to the large amount of debentures redeemed during the year which were not funded by any issue of long-term capital. In addition there was also substantial investment in fixed assets. In order to fund the shortfall the company obtained a bank overdraft and this switch to short-term finance has led to a poor liquidity position. There was also a reduction in other working capital items most markedly in the level of trade creditors and it seems that the company may have been placed on cash on delivery terms by its suppliers.

14 Short- and medium-term sources of finance

Introduction

The contents of this chapter are mainly descriptive, giving a guide to the short- and medium-term funds available to firms. However, the chapter contains an important section of a more analytic nature on **leasing** which has increased significantly in recent years as a method of project finance.

The short- and medium-term labels must of course be treated with discretion as there is almost inevitably some overlap between what is described as medium-term and long-term. As a rule of thumb, definition funds borrowed for up to one year may be regarded as short-term while one to five year borrowing can be viewed as medium-term.

Short-term bank borrowing

Bank overdrafts operate by extending a line of credit on the account holder's current account, thus enabling him to continue drawing cheques when funds are exhausted. Any payments into the account reduce the amount of the overdraft and interest is paid on a day-to-day basis on the balance outstanding. The account holder can draw funds up to the previously agreed overdraft limit. Because interest is paid on the fluctuating balance, this can make the overdraft a comparatively cheap form of short-term finance. However, overdrafts are repayable on demand by the bank and therefore too much reliance on the overdraft can make the trader vulnerable to changes in credit policy. Overdrafts should essentially be used for short-term finite requirements but there is a tendency, particularly for smaller companies, to regard them as a more or less permanent part of the capital structure, which can lead to problems.

With large blue chip companies, banks may be prepared to offer overdrafts without security, but it is usual for them to require either a fixed or floating charge on company assets as security. In the case of smaller private companies a personal guarantee from the owners is often required. The per annum interest rate is usually 2% to 5% above the bank's 'base rate', but because it is computed on the fluctuating balance, rather than a fixed sum, it is often cheaper than an equivalent fixed loan carrying the same rate of interest.

Bridging loans are available from banks for limited periods of time. They are commonly used to cover the time between the exchange of a contract and the eventual completion of a property sale. The cost might be a point or two higher than an overdraft and in addition a commitment fee may be payable. Unless the loan is in the form of an overdraft, interest will be paid on the full amount of the loan advanced.

Trade credit

Trade credit is an important form of short-term finance to companies. It represents the time taken for a buying company to pay a supplier and provided the period taken to pay does not extend beyond the normally agreed time, there is no direct interest charge. However, there can be an opportunity cost in that discounts are often offered for early payment and the loss of this discount must be compared with the potential interest saving on the period of extended credit.

Terms of credit vary from industry to industry each establishing its own accepted norm. Factors affecting length of credit are:

1. The type of product — those with a high sales turnover are generally sold on shorter credit terms than those with a lower sales turnover. However, there can be variations depending upon the importance of the buyer to the supplier concerned.
2. If the seller has a weak liquid position then he might find it difficult to offer long credit terms. However, if his competitors are offering better terms it will put pressure on the supplier to compete and he may have to improve his liquid position by other means.
3. If the buyer's liquid position is weak then he may seek to take a longer period of credit. However, suppliers may be deterred from dealing with this kind of customer and again credit might have to be obtained so as not to jeopardize the flow of supplies to the business.
4. Where cash discounts are offered for prompt payment and the cost of taking credit beyond the discount date may be high. The higher the cash discount offered the smaller the average trade credit is likely to be.

Bills and acceptances

Bills of exchange are now mainly used in connection with overseas trade. The bill is somewhat analogous to a post-dated cheque in that a bill requires the person to whom it is addressed to pay a sum at some future date. The bill is a negotiable instrument and the holder, usually the seller of goods, can obtain immediate funds by discounting the bill for a lower sum than the face value which will depend upon the length of time to maturity and the standing of the acceptor of the bill.

Acceptance credits have similarities with bills of exchange. The trader can obtain finance by drawing a bill of exchange on a bank. The bank accepts the bill, therefore committing itself to pay the face value at some future date. Because the bill is backed by the bank's reputation it can be sold in the money markets at a lower discount rate than a bill carrying the name of a trading company. The company drawing the bill must, of course, be creditworthy as the bank will wish to ensure that repayment will be made as and when due. From the company's point of view, acceptance credits are similar in nature to a medium-term overdraft and their cost can be cheaper than overdrafts. Acceptance credits are usually for comparatively large amounts — in excess of £250 000.

Debt factoring and discounting

Factoring involves raising funds on the security of the company's debts so that cash is received earlier than if the company waited for the debtors to pay. Clearing banks through their subsidiaries carry out most of the business in this area. Three basic services are offered.

1. Sales ledger accounting: invoicing and collection of accounts.
2. Credit insurance guaranteeing against bad debts.
3. Provision of finance by advancing funds of up to 80% of the value of debts being collected.

Customers can choose which of these services are required. Costs are generally based on a percentage of turnover handled with separate costs for each service provided. Factoring tends to be a comparatively expensive way of providing funds and companies should generally try and obtain funds through a bank before turning to this particular source.

Invoice discounting and **credit insurance** is a financial arrangement which benefits the liquidity position of the user. A company converts an invoice into cash by discounting the invoice through a specialized finance company. Either separate invoices can be discounted or a proportion of the total book debts. The potential borrower may find that the lender will be more willing to make the advance if the debt is insured. A premium is paid for this service as with any other type of insurance and this will depend on the amount involved and the perceived risks attached to the debt. Again this is a more costly form of providing finance than borrowing and both this and the factoring previously discussed are sometimes seen as borrowing of last resort.

Tax payments

A deferred tax payment is a source of short-term funds similar to trade credit but in this case it is supplied by tax authorities. The credit is created by the gap between the earning of profits and the payment of the taxes due on them. Under the corporation tax system the tax liability for a financial year does not have to be paid until a minimum of nine months has elapsed and in the case of some older companies as long as 21 months.

No interest has to be paid on this credit provided payments are made by the due dates.

Medium-term funds

Medium-term bank borrowing is now offered by all the major banks. Indeed following criticism of the facilities offered by banks in the 1960s, loans for even longer periods up to 20 years are now offered. The interest rate is usually variable between 2% and 5% above the bank's base rate. In addition an arrangement fee of up to $1\frac{1}{2}$% may also have to be paid to the bank. The amount borrowed could be as low as £2000 or as high as £250 000.

Government guaranteed loans were established in the UK in 1981 by the government to encourage bankers to lend money to businesses which might face difficulty in obtaining loans in the normal course of business. With this scheme the government guarantees to pay the bank 70% of the money outstanding should the customer not be able to repay. The banker may not take any personal security from the borrower, who is expected to pledge all the business assets as security for the loan. Loans may be from two to seven years and the government makes a 3% charge on top of the normal interest rate for the guarantee. The maximum loan under this scheme is £75 000. The scheme has proved to be popular but is not above criticism — the proportion of bad debts is high because it is said banks only take the riskier projects into the government scheme. In addition the total interest charge is seen to be high because of the additional guarantee charge required.

Merchant banks were historically seen as providers of risk capital, whereas the clearing banks were seen more as providers of loans. In fact the division between different financial institutions is becoming much less clear as the clearing banks have all formed merchant banking subsidiaries and there is a tendency within the City generally for large multi-service organizations to be formed. However, merchant banks still have a reputation for being more prepared to advance finance packages including equity stakes to expanding private companies.

Where a company obtains finance for exporting goods they are usually required to obtain insurance from the Export Credits Guarantee Department (ECGD) to cover the risks. The ECGD is a government department which helps export companies and issues guarantees appropriate to the terms of sale. With these guarantees the exporting company can borrow from a bank. The ECGD underwrites between 30% and 40% of all British exports and with an ECGD guarantee companies' bankers are willing to advance up to 100% of the value of an invoice under the 'bills and notes' scheme and up to 90% of the value of an invoice for trading on open account.

Project finance is a form of medium-term borrowing where the funds are advanced on a project basis rather than on the standing or potential of the borrower. This type of finance grew in importance during the 1970s, particularly in international business. Much of the North Sea oil developments were funded with this type of finance. Because of the

project basis and the risky nature of many of the projects a large proportion of project finance comes from official or quasi-official organizations.
The biggest single source of project finance is said to be the World Bank.

Hire purchase is a popular source of medium-term credit used for the
purchase of plant and equipment. Initially a hire purchase company purchases the equipment and immediately hires it to the company requiring
the equipment. The hiree makes a series of regular payments and at the
conclusion of the agreement has the option to purchase the equipment
for a nominal sum. The legal title to the equipment does not pass to the
hiree until the completion of the agreement. Hire purchase tends to be
an expensive form of finance, significantly more expensive, for example,
than bank borrowing. Unlike leasing which is considered later the eventual
purchasing company (the hiree) is entitled to claim tax relief in respect of
the capital allowances. It can also obtain tax relief on the interest element
in the payments it makes.

Sale and lease-back is a financing strategy whereby a company owning
valuable property assets obtains funds by selling the property but continues to use the assets by entering into immediate lease-back from the
financial intermediary. This type of arrangement experienced an increase
in popularity in the mid 1970s due to the shortage of investment opportunity available for institutions and insurance companies who have been
the principal providers of funds in this area. From a trading company's
viewpoint it obtains funds without taking on additional debt but, of
course, the fixed asset is replaced by cash. Any future capital gain will,
of course, accrue to the financing company, but it is sometimes argued
that the trading company is not in the business of owning property and
the funds released should earn a higher return in the business in which
it is engaged.

Mortgaging property is an alternative to sale and lease-back. Again
institutions such as insurance companies are the most likely providers of
funds. The main advantage of the mortgage is that the company retains
ownership of the property and therefore gains the benefit of any capital
appreciation. However, from a cash flow point of view, as capital repayment will be involved as well as interest the combined annual cost
is likely to be higher than the initial rentals payable under a sale and
lease-back arrangement.

Leasing

Leasing as a source of finance has increased in importance in recent
years. The **lessee** has the use of the asset and makes a series of periodic
payments to the owner of the asset, the **lessor**. **Operating leases** are
short-term and cancellable during the contract period at the option of the
lessee. For example, we might rent a TV or video under an operating
lease. **Financial leases** extend over the economic life of the asset and are
non-cancellable or only cancellable under penalty.

Why do companies lease?

1. An asset may only be required for a short period of time and in these
   circumstances short-term leasing makes sense. For example, many

items of plant used in the construction industry are only required for a short period of time and an operating lease is the best way of providing such plant.

2. Where high technology equipment is being used an operating lease can be valuable because of the option to cancel. In this way the costs of obsolescence are borne by the lessor who is usually the manufacturer and thus able to reflect potential obsolescence in the lease payments charged.

3. By far the most significant factor in the growth of financial leasing has been the ability to make earlier use of valuable tax shields. During the last decade many manufacturing companies have been in a permanent or semi-permanent non-tax-paying position. This has meant that when they have purchased capital equipment they have been unable to make use of the tax shield on the capital allowances. With a financial lease the lessor as owner of the plant can claim the allowance and make an offset against mainstream corporation tax liability. The lease instalments are fixed to reflect the allowances gained and thus the net cost to the lessee can be lower than the equivalent borrow-and-buy strategy.

4. Leasing has been cited as providing 'off balance sheet financing', that is a firm buys an asset, finances it through a financial lease and shows neither the asset nor the lease contract on its balance sheet. However, the ASC introduced a standard in 1984 which means that finance leases have to be capitalized. The leased asset appears on one side of the balance sheet, the liability on the other. Similar disclosure requirements were introduced in the USA in 1977. Despite the recent requirement to capitalize leases it is still questionable whether financiers and other users of accounts were ever fooled by the non-inclusion of assets and equivalent loans on balance sheets.

5. It was also claimed that leasing made book income look better as the lease payments in the early years were less than the depreciation plus interest which would be shown under the buy-and-borrow alternative. When this was combined with the balance sheet effect prior to capitalization the return on capital figure was said to be improved. Again this is entirely cosmetic rather than economic.

Lease evaluation adopts the same principles as the evaluation of any other asset. The incremental cash flows arising as a consequence of leasing are discounted at a rate appropriate to the level of risk; this rate is typically assumed to be r^*, given by

$$r^* = r(1 - t_c L_j)$$

where r^* adjusted discount rate;

r opportunity cost of capital borrowed for a similar deal;

t_c marginal corporation tax rate;

L_j particular leasing deal's proportional contribution to the company's borrowing power.

If leasing is regarded as displacing debt on a one for one basis then L_j would equal one in the above equation and r^* would be the after tax cost of borrowing.

The net present value of leasing from the lessee's viewpoint can be written as:

NPV = + Financing saved by leasing − PV of lease payments
+ PV of tax shield on lease payments − PV of tax
shield on capital allowances foregone by leasing rather
than buying − PV of after tax residual value

The NPV from the lessor's point of view will be as for the lessee with the signs reversed; that is outflows for the lessee are inflows for the lessor and vice versa. We will now examine an example where the choice of financing is under appraisal. An APV approach is adopted, first calculating the base case NPV of the project and then the NPV of leasing. The appraisal is considered first without tax and then taking tax into account.

Example

Colin, who runs a small engineering company, has discovered an investment opportunity, a new welding machine. He obtains the following estimates in connection with the installation of this machine:

Annual net revenue	£35 000
(received in cash at the end of each year of operation)	
Initial outlay — total purchase price	£120 000
— leasing	£20 000
Lease payments (payable at the end of each of the	
next 5 years)	£24 000
Useful life of the machine	5 years

Colin is not sure if he should go ahead. He knows he could raise finance to buy the machine by borrowing from his bank at 10%, or selling some of the shares he holds in a publicly quoted company earning 15% and considered to be of the same risk as the welding machine opportunity. The salesman of the welding machines offers to summarize the problem and carries out the calculations given below:

	£	£
Annual revenue	35 000	
Annual lease payments	24 000	
Annual net revenue	11 000	
Initial outlay for lease		20 000
15% on above initial outlay	3 000	
Annual benefits from leasing welding machine	£8 000	

You are required to recommend to Colin whether he should have the machine installed or not. Show calculations in arriving at your recommendation, identifying any important assumptions.

Solution

The rationale for the saleman's statement is difficult to understand, particularly the treatment of initial outlay for the lease. There would seem to be no theoretical support for the calculation of benefits and an appraisal should be made using DCF techniques.

No reference is made to taxation so an appraisal will be made first of all assuming no tax implications.

$$\text{Base case NPV of project} = -120\,000 + \sum_{t=1}^{5} \frac{35\,000}{(1 + r)^t}$$

Using a risk-adjusted discount rate of 15%,

$$\begin{aligned} \text{NPV} &= -120\,000 + 35\,000\ (3.3522) \\ &= -2673 \end{aligned}$$

Now consider NPV of leasing,

$$\text{NPV leasing} = +120\,000 - 20\,000 - \sum_{t=1}^{5} \frac{24\,000}{(1 + r)^t}$$

Using a borrowing rate of 10% to discount cash flows,

$$\begin{aligned} \text{NPV} &= +120\,000 - 20\,000 - 24\,000\ (3.7908) \\ &= +9021 \\ \text{APV} &= -2673 + 9021 \\ &= +6348 \end{aligned}$$

Although the project on its own has a negative NPV when combined with the profitable leasing deal we get an overall positive APV.

Now assume that capital allowances of 25% on a straight line basis are available and corporation tax is 35%. Further assume that tax benefits/ liabilities are lagged by one year and that the project required return remains at 15%:

$$\begin{aligned} \text{Base case NPV} &= -120\,000 + \sum_{t=1}^{4} \frac{120\,000 \times 0.25 \times 0.35}{(1 + 0.15)^t} \\ &\quad + \sum_{t=1}^{5} \frac{35\,000}{(1 + 0.15)^t} - \sum_{t=2}^{6} \frac{35\,000 \times 0.35}{(1 + 0.15)^t} \\ &= -120\,000 + 10\,500\ (2.8550) + 35\,000\ (3.3522) \\ &\quad - 12\,250\ (3.3522)\ (0.8696) \\ &= -8405 \end{aligned}$$

With tax the after-tax cost of borrowing is assumed to be $10(1 - 0.35) = 6.5\%$ and this is used in the calculation below:

$$\begin{aligned} \text{NPV leasing} &= +120\,000 - \sum_{t=1}^{4} \frac{120\,000 \times 0.25 \times 0.35}{(1 + 0.065)} - 20\,000 \\ &\quad - \sum_{t=1}^{5} \frac{24\,000}{(1 + 0.065)^t} + \frac{20\,000 \times 0.35}{(1 + 0.065)} \\ &\quad + \sum_{t=2}^{6} \frac{24\,000 \times 0.35}{(1 + 0.065)^t} \\ &= +3642 \\ \text{APV} &= -8405 + 3642 \\ &= -4763 \end{aligned}$$

With taxation, leasing becomes less profitable. This is because the lessee now loses the tax allowance on capital expenditure and the lease payments become more expensive because of the lower discount rate used; these are partially offset by the tax shield on the lease payments. The base case NPV of the project also falls because the PV of the tax on profits is greater than the PV of the capital allowances. Thus with tax the APV is negative and the project not worthwhile, however financed. This example also emphasizes that leasing becomes more valuable if the lessee does not pay tax and has lower tax rates than the lessor.

15 Management of cash

Introduction

Cash management is as important both to the survival and value maximization of the firm as the management of any other asset or liability. If the firm cannot take advantage of profitable opportunities or meet its obligations as they fall due because of the absence of cash, it runs the risk, at the best, of reducing profit or, at the worst, being put into liquidation. Efficient cash management can both ensure the solvency of the firm and add to its value.

Cash management seeks to achieve a balance between too little and too much cash. Essentially the manager forgoes interest on cash which could otherwise be invested in exchange for liquidity.

In carrying cash the manager is able to take advantage of discounts offered by suppliers for prompt payment, in general debts can be met as they fall due and the company is in a position to take advantage of any investment opportunities requiring cash. On the other hand, if resources are tied up in cash not earning a return, it must mean there are fewer resources engaged in a profitable activity.

The cost of carrying cash to the firm is like any other cost, an opportunity cost. If the firm has sufficient liquid funds to enable short-term investments to be made then the cost is the return on the alternative investment forgone. On the other hand, if the firm is funding its short-term requirements through a bank overdraft then the appropriate cost is the cost in interest terms of the overdraft.

Cash budgets

Cash budgets play an essential part in successful cash management. The cash coming into and going out of the firm is likely to vary month by month. This is particularly so where the pattern of trade is uneven throughout the year, perhaps because of its seasonal nature. A cash budget sets out the monthly, or if required, weekly, projections of cash to be received and paid together with the projected cash balance at the end of the month or week. In this way the times of the year when cash will be available and the times when short-term loans may be required can be identified in advance. The existence of a cash budget will be a normal prerequisite for both obtaining and managing facilities made available by the firm's bankers.

A firm may be able to improve its cash position through a better system of depositing sums received. This may be particularly so with a firm that has divisional offices. A small company may only deposit funds at the bank once or twice a week. By making more frequent deposits the firm may be able to save on overdraft interest or else have positive cash balances with which to make short-term deposits. This has become increasingly important with the high levels of interest rates existing in recent years. However, it must be borne in mind that more frequent bankings may involve an extra cost and it is necessary to compare the benefit of more frequent or earlier bankings with the additional costs involved in making them.

Float represents the money arising from the time lag between the date on which a cheque is sent through the post to the time it is eventually cleared by the recipient's bank. This time delay can be between four and nine days depending on the postal service, time taken to pay in cheque, time taken to clear cheque by bank and any delays due to weekends and bank holidays. From a supplier's point of view it might be possible to reduce the size of the float by the use of direct debits on customers' accounts. However, the payee will naturally try and increase the size of the float tied up in his payments to suppliers either to minimize overdraft levels or enable liquid funds to be invested for a longer term.

Product life cycle must be considered in determining cash needs. Products in their early stages of development of production will generally be consuming cash both in terms of capital costs and initial working capital. There will then be a growth in positive cash flows followed by a lower level of positive cash flows as the product reaches the end of its life cycle. It is therefore essential that cash requirements, particularly in the early stages of the life cycle, be carefully planned.

We will now illustrate the importance of cash budgets in planning the future financial policies of a business with an example.

Example
A friend has asked for your advice as follows:

I am thinking of establishing the Northern Sales Agency for some highly specialized — and expensive — scientific instruments. I am convinced that the profits eventually will be really big but I am not certain about the first year. I have shares which currently have a sales value of £10 000 and that will certainly cover the initial advertising and sales promotion which will be required. I will not need any premises because I intend working from my home — where my wife will look after the clerical work — but the extra telephone, stationery, expenses, etc. will be about £100 a month. In addition, all stocks will be held by the main distributor in London who will deliver direct to my customers so there will be no storage requirements. In the first year sales will be at least £144 000 and there is no reason why they should not increase substantially thereafter. With a gross profit percentage of 25%, therefore the £36 000 in the first year will pay for the sample instruments I will have to carry around in my car to show to customers. Fortunately, I already own my car so there will be no expense other than petrol and oil, etc. which according to the last AA report I read should work out about 20p per mile. My business mileage will be between 10 000 and 15 000 miles per annum and of course I appreciate that the running expenses for this will have to be paid for in cash.

I will give my customers the usual trade terms, i.e. they will have to pay me at the end of the month following the month in which they receive the goods but given the current economic situation some may take an extra month. The money from sales won't come in evenly of course because in the middle two quarters of the year sales will be twice what they are in the other two quarters. I am not sure when I will have to pay the main distributor after he supplies my customers; I know that down South it is within one week of delivery and when they say one week that is what they mean — but in the early stages they have indicated that they will be more lenient as I have got to pay the agency acquisition fee of £20 000 plus 1% commission on all sales, payable quarterly in arrears. The initial acquisition fee lasts for five years so after this first payment all I will have is the sales commission charge and then eventually a new deal will have to be negotiated. Do you think there will be enough profits to let me pay my way during the first year?

You are required to draft a statement showing:

1. the level of profit anticipated for the first year (assume the year consists of 12 four-weekly periods);
2. a cash budget for the first year by quarters;
3. why profit is not synonymous with cash and why in terms of your client's ability to survive the first 12 months a cash flow budget with appropriate quarterly figures is required;
4. a comment on (1) and (2) including the other information you would like to have in order to provide a more satisfactory answer to these.

Solution guide

1.   Estimated profit

Sales		£144 000
Less: cost of sales (75%)		108 000
		36 000
Car expenses (15 000 × 20p)	3 000	
Telephone etc. (£100 × 12)	1 200	
Agency fee (£20 000 ÷ 5)	4 000	
Commission	1 440	
Advertising/promotion	10 000	19 640
Net profit		£16 360

This ignores any wages which the wife might earn and any depreciation on the car.

2. *Estimated cash budget for first year*

			Quarter		
Cash in	*1*	*2*	*3*	*4*	*Total*
Sales	16 000	40 000	48 000	32 000	136 000
Sales of Shares	10 000				10 000
	26 000	40 000	48 000	32 000	146 000
Cash out					
Advertising etc.	10 000				10 000
Car expenses	750	750	750	750	3 000
Telephone	300	300	300	300	1 200
Agency fees	20 000				20 000
Commission	360	360	360	360	1 440
Purchases	16 500	34 500	36 000	19 500	106 500
Sample instruments	36 000				36 000
	83 910	35 910	37 410	20 910	178 140
Quarterly Cash surplus/ deficit	−57 910	+4 090	+10 590	+11 090	
Cash balance	−57 910	−53 820	−43 230	−32 140	

Notes on cash budget

Sales

The sales for the first and last quarter will be half that for the second and third. One-sixth of the annual sales will therefore be made in the first and last quarters with two-sixths in the second and third.

If it is assumed that only one month of sales will be owing at the end of each quarter then cash received in each quarter will be calculated as follows:

	1	2	3	4
Sales per quarter	24 000	48 000	48 000	24 000
Cash received				
$\frac{2}{3} \times 24\,000$	16 000			
$\frac{1}{3} \times 24\,000$		8 000		
$\frac{2}{3} \times 48\,000$		32 000		
$\frac{1}{3} \times 48\,000$			16 000	
$\frac{2}{3} \times 48\,000$			32 000	
$\frac{1}{3} \times 48\,000$				16 000
$\frac{2}{3} \times 24\,000$				16 000
	16 000	40 000	48 000	32 000

Purchases

The purchases per month will be 75% of sales. All but one week's purchases will be paid each quarter.

Purchases per quarter	<u>18 000</u>	<u>36 000</u>	<u>36 000</u>	<u>18 000</u>
Cash paid	16 500			
$18\,000 \times \frac{11}{12}$				
$18\,000 \times \frac{1}{12}$		1 500		
$36\,000 \times \frac{11}{12}$		33 000		
$36\,000 \times \frac{1}{12}$			3 000	
$36\,000 \times \frac{11}{12}$			33 000	
$36\,000 \times \frac{1}{12}$				3 000
$18\,000 \times \frac{11}{12}$				16 500
	<u>16 500</u>	<u>34 500</u>	<u>36 000</u>	<u>19 500</u>

Commission

It could be argued that as the question says commission payable quarterly in arrears, no cash payment should appear in the first quarter. This would have only a very small effect on the cash balances.

3. Profit is not synonymous with cash, because certain items deducted to arrive at profit for a year are not the same as the cash outflows for the year. Depreciation is not a cash outflow but is deducted from profit, the cash outflow being the capital expenditure. Accrual accounting charges expenses to a period when the benefit is received and recognizes income when earned, which can differ from the respective cash flows. The cash budget shows that even though the business may be profitable over the year, there is a large initial net cash outflow to be met, and the quarterly inflows only slowly reduce this cash outlay. Arrangements will have to be made with a bank, or some other source, to provide the finance needed.

4. Further information is needed on the taxation position of the business, a possible salary for the wife, the life of the car, any possible bad debts or late payers, and any further sales promotions or investments in storage facilities.

Short-term investments

Short-term investment opportunities will be revealed by the use of cash budgets and the careful monitoring of the cash resources available to the company. In any circumstances any surplus funds not immediately required should be invested. However, this is of particular importance due to the high interest rates that have been available in recent years. Important factors in determining the type of investment are

1. size of the amounts available;
2. period for which the cash is available;
3. likelihood cash may be required prematurely to make unexpected payments.

Investments should be geared to get maximum interest possible consistent with a low risk and high liquidity or negotiability. These are usually short-term funds which the company is likely to call upon at short notice to meet its trading obligations and therefore these are important factors. Should there be a semi-permanent surplus of cash funds within the company then a different strategy giving consideration to longer term securities would be necessary.

The largest proportion of short-term funds are deposited with the banking sector on terms ranging from call (available immediately) to three months. Although it would normally be expected that the longer the deposit the higher the rate of interest would be, this would depend on current market conditions and the current term structure of interest rates.

Certificates of deposit are negotiable certificates issued by a bank when a deposit is made, usually for a minimum of three months and a maximum of five years. Because there is an active secondary market with these deposits they make attractive short-term investments for firms with large sums of money to invest.

Tax reserve certificates may also be a useful short-term investment. A company may wish to provide funds for a future tax bill and the purchase of these certificates enables interest to be earned up to the time the certificate is surrendered in full or part payment of the tax liability. These certificates offer an attractive rate of interest but it should not noted that if they are surrendered for cash the rate of interest earned is substantially less.

British government securities such as treasury bills are issued on behalf of central government to fund their cash needs and can be purchased and sold through the money market. In addition, there are also quoted government securities which may be purchased and sold through the Stock Market. Dealing is for cash settlement and the shorter term maturities might be suitable investments for short-term cash.

Local authority bonds can be purchased with a maturity of anything from two days to five years. The company could buy a bond with a life span relating to the availability of surplus funds. However, local authority bonds have a lower level of liquidity than many other investment options and the market for them is small.

The financial manager needs to maintain liquidity but not excess liquidity. Some cash or near cash has to be available, but where liquid assets are substantial a portfolio should be constructed with securities of varying maturities ranging from overnight money to a number of months. This portfolio should be constructed using the cash budget as a guide to future cash requirements and taking into consideration market conditions.

16 Management of debtors

Introduction

UK companies have a considerable proportion of their funds invested in debtors, in the region of 20% to 25%. Compared with other countries, notably the USA, the average time taken to collect debts is significantly longer. The average UK company takes about 60 days to collect debts while in the USA it is in the region of 40 days. Although it could be that a more professional approach towards credit management is adopted in the USA than in the UK, it could also reflect cultural differences towards paying debts between the two countries.

Credit policy

A number of factors will affect a company's policy towards the credit terms extended to its customers, amongst them being

1. The terms on which goods are to be sold. A decision must be taken on how long customers are to be given to pay bills and also if cash discount is to be offered for prompt payment. If the company operates in an established industry there are likely to be trade norms established both in terms of credit given and discounts allowed. In these circumstances it will be difficult for the company to offer worse terms than competing companies and there will be a tendency to base terms on those currently in use in the industry.
2. The company must decide which companies it intends to deal with. Is a judgment to be made on the basis of the customer's past records or past financial statements? Or will a customer's suitability be determined on the basis of a bank reference or credit agency rating?
3. The amount of credit to be extended to each customer must be determined. Is it to be company policy to deal only with established organizations with a sound track record? Or is it acceptable to take the risk of some bad debts in an effort to obtain more customers, even though they may include some companies of doubtful financial reputation?
4. After credit has been granted and sales made, a system of collection must be implemented. This system must enable collection to be made

in line with the terms previously determined and must include procedures for dealing with slow payers.

Each of the factors will have implications for the firm's liquidity and profitability. For example, the longer the credit terms the greater the amount of debtors and the greater the possible strain on the company's liquidity. In addition, longer credit terms will involve a larger investment in debtors and there will be an opportunity cost in terms of alternative investment forgone. We will now examine each of the above four factors in more detail.

The credit terms and conditions of sale will often be determined by the usual terms of trade of the particular industry. Most of the trade credit granted in the UK is on monthly terms, payment being required on or before the last day of the month following the date of the invoice, e.g. goods despatched during March will be due for payment by the end of April.

Cash discounts have traditionally been offered by the seller to the buyer to encourage payment before the end of the period of credit. Cash discounts can be analysed in terms of both costs and benefit to seller and buyer. The seller forgoes a small percentage of the sale price in order to obtain earlier access to the sale proceeds which will benefit him in terms of lower bank overdraft interest or higher interest received on the funds invested. On the other hand, the buyer obtains the benefit of the discount but suffers an opportunity cost in terms of interest forgone. Problems on whether or not to offer cash discount, or indeed take cash discount, can be analysed on this basis.

Credit risk

Every sale on credit involves some risk that the customer will not be able to pay. With most large companies the risk is likely to be considered insignificant. However, other companies might appear to be such bad risks that they will not be considered as potential customers. Between these two extremes the company will have to make decisions on whether to sell on credit or not. The credit manager might split potential customers into groups with different credit risk ratings to make decision making easier. Again it will be a cost benefit calculation involving setting off the expected value of bad debts against the incremental benefit to be derived from additional sales. The cost structure of the company may well be an important factor in reaching this decision. A company with high fixed costs will gain a larger contribution per pound of sale than one with a high proportion of variable costs and may well feel that it is able to take on customers with a higher potential risk level.

Assessing the risk of a potential customer is not easy. However, the following sources of information may be useful:

1. **Trade references.** A new customer could be required to supply one or two references from other companies with whom they have had business.
2. **Bank references.** A bank may be requested to comment on the fin-

ancial standing of its customer. A banker's comment on one of its own customers is only of limited use. The reference tends to be of a standard form and very carefully worded, sometimes so hedged that it adds very little.

3. **Credit bureaux, reports or registers.** A number of sources are available in the UK, e.g. Dunn and Bradstreet. These companies publish lists of companies showing relevant financial details including a credit rating. There is a continuing growth of information becoming available in connection with trading organizations and it is to be expected that the boom in information technology will soon provide data-based sources of information which will be available on a subscription basis.

4. **Published accounts.** As well as annual accounts which can be analysed to determine the liquidity position of the customer the Registrar of Companies keeps records of charges on the assets of the company and other details. One problem with both these sources is that in the case of ailing companies, preparation and filing of information may well be in arrears, making the publicly available information somewhat out of date.

Credit limits and debt collection

The amount of credit to be extended to each customer will be dependent to some extent on factors already discussed above. A particular problem to the credit manager will be regular customers who pay late and require additional credit above a previously agreed level. This effectively means extending that customer's credit limit. Should the credit manager refuse further supplies until payment is made, thus running the risk of losing the customers? Or should the credit manager go on with the effectively increased credit limit? There are really no easy answers. Each case needs to be treated on merits and judgment exercised. The objective should be profit maximization and the manager must weigh the benefit of receiving additional revenues against the potential bad debts which might be incurred by extending credit.

A debt collection policy must be implemented. When the sale has been made the company will try to ensure that the cash is received as soon as it is due. Unfortunately not all customers pay their bills on time! The credit manager will keep a record of payment relating to each customer and will periodically draw up a schedule showing the age of accounts receivable. This will highlight any customers in arrears.

There should be a stated procedure for dealing with customers in arrears. Initially it is common practice to send a statement of account, and if payment is still not made, follow this with increasingly pointed reminders and telephone calls. If these measures are not successful then the company might threaten legal action or hand the debt over to a collection agency. The latter measures incur significant costs and the company will always seek to collect the debt without recourse to either agency or solicitor.

Credit insurance can be taken out where the company is concerned about non-payment of accounts. Specialist companies provide this insurance but as may be expected, premiums are high. In addition the credit insurance company may refuse to take on debtors it sees as high risk. Either **whole turnover** or **specific account insurance** is available.

We will now illustrate the costs and benefits of alternative strategies using an examination question taken from the ICAEW.

Problem

Blue Jays Ltd manufactures several types of knitwear, which it sells to a variety of retail outlets. The company expects to suffer a temporary shortage of funds during the first three months of 1984 and its directors are considering three alternative means of meeting the shortfall, as follows:

1.   Delay payments to trade creditors in respect of purchases of wool. At present, Blue Jays Ltd receives a cash discount of $2\frac{1}{2}\%$ in return for settlement of creditors' invoices within one month of the invoice date. It takes advantage of this discount in respect of all invoices received. The proposed policy would involve payment of 50% of invoices (by value) at the end of two months and 50% at the end of three months.

2.   Offer discounts to trade debtors. At present, Blue Jays Ltd offers no cash discount for early settlement of invoices. On average, 10% of debtors pay one month after invoice date, 36% two months after invoice date and 50% three months after invoice date. Four per cent of trade debts are bad. The proposed policy would be to offer a discount of 3% for payment within one month of the invoice date. If the policy were implemented, the directors expect that 50% of debtors would pay one month after invoice date, 22% two months after invoice date and 25% three months after invoice date. Three per cent of trade debts would be bad.

3.   Undertake short-term borrowing. Overdraft facilities are available from the company's bankers at an interest cost of 1% per month. Short-term borrowing could be undertaken to meet all of the expected shortfall or just the shortfall remaining after the implementation of either or both of the two alternatives described above.

If either of the first two alternatives were adopted, it would be applied only to invoices received or issued in January, February and March 1984. Thereafter, Blue Jays Ltd would revert to its existing policies.

The actual and expected sales of Blue Jays Ltd for the nine months from October 1983 to June 1984 are as follows:

			£
Actual sales	October	1983	250 000
	November	1983	250 000
Expected sales	December	1983	200 000
	January	1984	200 000
	February	1984	160 000
	March	1984	140 000
	April	1984	140 000
	May	1984	140 000
	June	1984	160 000

Wool is purchased, and the manufacture of knitwear takes place, in the month before sale. For all types of knitwear, the cost of wool is equal to 30% of selling price. All invoices for sales or purchases are issued or received by Blue Jays Ltd on the last day of the month to which they relate.

You are required to

1. Prepare calculations showing the effect on the cash flows of Blue Jays Ltd on a month by month basis if the company
   (a) delays payments to creditors in respect of January, February and March wool purchased; (5 marks)
   (b) offers discounts to trade debtors in respect of January, February and March sales. (5 marks)
2. Prepare calculations showing whether either delaying payments to creditors or offering discounts to debtors is worthwhile. (5 marks)
3. Draft a note for the directors of Blue Jays Ltd advising them on any matters not included in your calculations in (1) and (2) above, which they should consider in arriving at their decision on whether to change temporarily their existing policies relating to trade creditors and trade debtors. (10 marks)

Note: Ignore taxation.

(ICAEW, Financial Management)

Solution

1. (a) Delaying payment to creditors:

   Expected purchases: 30% × next month's sales
   January   30% × £160 000 = £48 000
   February 30% × £140 000 = £42 000
   March   30% × £140 000 = £42 000

	Without policy	£	With policy	£	Incremental £
February	48 000 × 97½%	= 46 800			46 800
March	42 000 × 97½%	= 40 950		24 000	16 950
April	42 000 × 97½%	= 40 950	21 000 + 24 000 =	45 000	(4 050)
May			21 000 + 21 000 =	42 000	(42 000)
June				21 000	(21 000)

(b) Discounts to debtors:

Effect of scheme in percentage terms	Original %	New %	New − old %
One month after	10	48.50	38.50
Two months after	36	22	(14)
Three months after	50	25	(25)
	96	95.50	
Bad	4	3	
Discount	−	1.50	
	100	100.00	

	Jan sales £200 000	Feb sales £160 000	Mar sales £140 000	Total incremental cash flow
February	77 000			77 000
March	(28 000)	61 600		33 600
April	(50 000)	(22 400)	53 900	(18 500)
May		(40 000)	(19 600)	(59 600)
June			(35 000)	(35 000)

2.   PV of delaying payment to creditors:

$$\frac{46\,800}{(1.01)^2} + \frac{16\,950}{(1.01)^3} - \frac{4050}{(1.01)^4} - \frac{42\,000}{(1.01)^5} - \frac{21\,000}{(1.01)^6} = £(1307)$$

Negative net present value, therefore not worthwhile.
PV of offering discount to debtors:

$$\frac{77\,000}{(1.01)^2} + \frac{33\,600}{(1.01)^3} - \frac{18\,500}{(1.01)^4} - \frac{59\,600}{(1.01)^5} - \frac{35\,000}{(1.01)^6} = £638$$

Positive net present value, therefore worthwhile.
3.   Matters to be included in report:

(a)   *Creditors policy.* If payments are delayed to creditors relationship with suppliers may be disturbed. Supply and delivery of goods may suffer as creditors may favour other more prompt payers. Terms of trade may be altered to the company's detriment in terms of prices and discounts allowed. The creditor's business may suffer cash flow problems which in turn could affect future supply of goods.

(b)   *Debtors policy.* The computations assume payments are made on dates anticipated. With discount schemes, invariably some debtors take the discount while paying a few days (or even more) late. In addition, if the discount date is missed the debtor may take even longer to pay.

   Additional administrative costs would be incurred in introducing the scheme and in administering the type of problems raised above.

(c)   *General comments.* The benefit of the debtors policy over borrowing on overdraft is modest even before considering items raised in (b) above. It would be disruptive to change policies for only a short period of time and the flexibility offered by an overdraft facility would seem to offer the best solution.

17 Inventory management

Introduction

Inventory or stock control is an important aspect of working capital management. The investment in inventory may be substantial and can amount to as much as 20% to 40% of total business assets depending upon the type of industry.

The three main types of inventory are

1. **pre-production** (raw materials) inventory;
2. **in process** inventory (work in progress);
3. **finished goods.**

The main purposes of stock holding are

1. to enable customer order to be satisfied from stock;
2. to act as a buffer between stages of production;
3. to provide secure and regular supplies of materials;
4. to secure economies of scale in purchasing materials and semi-finished goods.

The best stock control policy is sought which will give decision rules for the size and timing of replenishments and procedure in stock-outs.

The classical model

The **classical static model** assumes:

1. a single item of stock;
2. all parameters known and constant;
3. instantaneous replenishment of stock;
4. no variable re-order costs.

Total costs in this model — sometimes called **relevant** or **controllable** costs — are given by

$$C = \frac{1}{2}QH + \frac{FD}{Q} \tag{17.1}$$

where Q is the quantity re-ordered, H is the holding costs per unit per annum, F is the fixed costs per re-order and D is annual demand. Costs are minimized for

$$\bar{Q} = \sqrt{\frac{2FD}{H}} \qquad (17.2)$$

$\bar{Q}$ is the **economic order quantity** (EOQ) or **economic lot size** (ELS) and (17.2) is known as the **square root rule**. $\bar{Q}$ is robust with respect to errors of estimation of parameters — an important practical advantage. When **unit costs** (U) are included an amount UD must be added to (17.1) but the square root rule is unchanged.

Problem
The annual demand for a company's single item of stock is 1000 units. It costs the company £6 to hold one unit of stock for one year. Each time that a replenishment order is made the company incurs a fixed cost of £75.

1. Determine the economic order quantity to two decimal places.
2. Suppose that the company's supplier of stock introduces a condition that normally there shall be no more than five orders for replenishment per annum. How much would the company be prepared to pay in order to avoid having to meet this condition?

Solution
$D = 1000, H = 6, F = 75$

$$\therefore \text{EOQ} = \sqrt{\frac{2 \times 75 \times 1000}{6}}$$
$$\therefore \bar{Q} = 158.11$$

This calls for $1000/158.11 = 6.32$ orders per annum (view this as a rate of ordering). Total costs are:

$$\frac{1}{2} \times 158.11 \times 6 + \frac{75 \times 1000}{158.11} = 474.33 + 474.35$$
$$= 948.68$$

With only five re-orders per annum, re-order size would be 200. Putting this value into the cost expression gives:

$$\frac{1}{2} \times 200 \times 6 + \frac{75 \times 1000}{200} = 600 + 375$$
$$= 975$$

The absolute maximum that the company would pay is £975 − £948.68 = £26.32.

Lead time and buffer stocks

Lead time (L) — the delay between ordering and arrival of stock — is allowed for by triggering the replenishment process when stock has fallen to the **re-order level** or re-order **point** (R). The re-order level model is often implemented as a **two bin** system. With **buffer stock** (B) (the average stock remaining at end of each **cycle**) added, the re-order level is given by

$$R = LW + B \qquad (17.3)$$

where W is weekly demand.

Where demand is a discrete random variable, enumeration may be used to determine the optimum buffer stock and hence re-order level from (17.3). The optimal buffer stock minimizes 'uncertainty costs' X where

$$X = BSHC + SOC \qquad (17.4)$$

In (17.4) BSHC is buffer stock holding costs and SOC is stock-out costs. The costs X are additional to the relevant costs in (17.1). An average value for annual demand is first used to determine the EOQ from (17.2) and hence the number of cycles. Then the buffer stock is calculated to minimize (17.4).

Sensitivity analysis can be conducted on the estimated shortage cost figure or, at greater complexity, on holding or other costs.

Service level approach

In **service level** approaches to stochastic demand, re-order level is set to provide a predetermined chance that customer orders can be satisfied from stock during the lead time. The $97\frac{1}{2}\%$ vendor service level is given by

$$R = LW + 1.96\sigma\sqrt{L} \qquad (17.5)$$

where σ is the standard deviation of weekly demand and where $1.96\sigma\sqrt{L}$ is the level of buffer stock. Sensitivity analysis is worthwhile on the stock-out cost figures. The **unit normal loss integral** or **service function** can also be used in a service level approach. Customer service level is defined as the percentage of demand met from stock (G) where

$$G = \frac{100Q - 19.78\sigma\sqrt{L}}{Q} \qquad (17.6)$$

In the **build up model** the length of **production run** is considered. With a production rate of P units per annum the EOQ is increased by the factor $\sqrt{P/(P - D)}$.

When **quantity discounts** (or economies of scale) affect the unit cost figure, the EOQ will be either at $\bar{Q}$ given by (17.2) or at one of the **price-break** points — the value of Q at which a lower unit cost takes effect — above the EOQ.

The classical static model can be used in cash management with procurement and interest costs being the analogues of replenishment costs and holding costs respectively.

Problem

Circa Holding Co. is examining its inventory policy in relation to one type of light-weight car wheel that it stores. Demand for the wheel runs at the average rate of 1000 units per quarter. It costs Circa £8 to hold one wheel for one year. When a re-order is necessary, Circa has fixed administrative costs of £40 irrespective of order size. The manufacturer charges Circa £12 per wheel supplied plus a charge of £120 no matter how large the order.

1. (a) Determine the economic order quantity.
    (b) An alternative scheme of charges would produce total costs per annum (including the £12 per wheel) of £52 000. Should Circa adopt the alternative scheme?
2. Assume a 50 week working year. Lead time is four weeks. Variance of demand in any week is 156.25 units. It can be assumed that demand in each week is normally distributed about the weekly average and is independent of demand in other weeks.
    (a) Determine the re-order level that would provide a $97\frac{1}{2}\%$ 'service level'.
    (b) Circa management, in an attempt to economize, is considering a reduction of the service level to 80%. Each stock-out is estimated to cost Circa £120. Is the planned reduction in service level advisable?

Solution

$D = 4000$, $H = 8$, $F = 160$, $U = 12$

$$\bar{Q} = \sqrt{\frac{2 \times 160 \times 4000}{8}} = 400$$

so that there will be 10 cycles per annum. The total cost at present is

$$4Q + \frac{640\,000}{Q} + 48\,000 = 51\,200$$

So that the alternative scheme should be rejected.

Now weekly demand is $4000 \div 50 = 80$ with variance 156.25 (i.e. standard deviation $= 12.5$). For a $97\frac{1}{2}\%$ vendor service level:

$$R = LW + 1.96\sigma\sqrt{L}$$
$$= 4 \times 80 + 1.96 \times 12.5 \times 2 = 369$$

At $97\frac{1}{2}\%$ service level the probability of a stock-out each cycle is 0.025, so that the expected number of stock-outs per annum is $0.025 \times 10 = 0.25$. The buffer stock is 49 here. At 80% service level the buffer stock is

$$B = 0.84\sigma\sqrt{L} = 21$$

The expected number of stock-outs per annum is $0.2 \times 10 = 2$. So, at the 80% level:

$$\begin{aligned} \text{BSHC} &= 21 \times 8 = & 168 \\ \text{SOC} &= 2 \times 120 = & \underline{240} \\ \text{Total} & & 408 \end{aligned}$$

Whereas at the $97\frac{1}{2}\%$ service level:

$$
\begin{array}{rl}
\text{BSHC} = 49 \times 8 = & 392 \\
\text{SOC} = 0.25 \times 120 = & \underline{30} \\
\text{Total} & 422
\end{array}
$$

so that the reduction in vendor service level is advisable on grounds of cost. Since stock-out is difficult to estimate a sensitivity analysis of the result is worthwhile. Instead of £120 let the stock-out cost be S. For the 80% service level to be preferable we require that

$$168 + 2S \leqslant 392 + 0.25S$$
$$\therefore S \leqslant 128$$

Thus only a $6\frac{2}{3}\%$ increase in S is tolerable. The result should therefore be regarded with caution.

Periodic review models

In inventory models with **periodic review**, stock-takings replace the constant monitoring required by the re-order level approach. If at the stock-taking inventory is at or below the re-order level a replenishment order of fixed size is placed – otherwise there is no re-ordering. In this periodic review model, information costs are reduced in comparison to the re-order level policy, but this is achieved at the expense of increased average stock level or increased stock-out costs.

In the **re-order cycle** model there is no re-order level and a replenishment order of size $S - I$ is placed at each review where I is the stock on hand at review and S is a predetermined maximum level. The re-order cycle model has the advantage of generally reducing stock-out costs but with increased re-order or holding costs in comparison to the periodic review model.

In the s, S model there is a periodic review with re-order level, s, at review. Re-order quantity is $S - I$. This model frequently gives the best results.

Zero inventory is optimal when it is cheaper to undertake **production to order**. Where batches of size X are ordered n times per year for

$$m = \sqrt{\frac{2nF}{XH}} \tag{17.7}$$

if $m < 1$ produce to order; if $m \geqslant 2$ stock the item; if $1 < m < 2$ further investigation is required.

The ABC classification system

In the **ABC classification** system (**Pareto analysis**), category A items (the 10% or so of product range that may account for 70%+ of total turnover) warrant detailed forecasting and stock control methods; category B items (say the 30% of product range accounting for 20% or so of turnover) warrant simple forecasting methods with robust estimates of EOQs;

category C items (the 60% of the product range that may account for just 10% of turnover) warrant basic methods only – say a two bin re-order system.

Lot size inventory management

In the **lot size inventory management technique** (LIMIT) account is taken of the cost of identifying holding costs. If holding cost H is expressable as a proportion h of unit costs U then the frequency of re-order should be N where

$$N = \sqrt{\frac{UD}{k}} \qquad (17.8)$$

where the parameter k is given by

$$k = \sqrt{\frac{2F}{h}}$$

In practice k may be estimated company-wide and substituted directly into (17.8).

Material Requirements Planning (MRP) methods and Just-in-Time management (JIT)

These methods can bring substantial reductions in stock-holding costs in manufacturing businesses where many components are assembled into a finished product. The motor vehicle industry is one where these methods have been implemented. Demand for the component parts is obtained from the forecast demand for the finished product and projected over time. As the individual requirements are specifically stated stocks of components, materials and work in progress can be substantially reduced. MRP requires a detailed production schedule and estimates of lead time for bought-out components. A computer-based MRP package will derive orders for components etc. from the production schedule.

MRP is central to manufacturing resource planning (MRP II) which is a comprehensive systems-oriented package including production, marketing and finance in high-volume complex manufacturing companies (e.g. motor vehicles). Procurement orders and delivery timings are derived from orders for finished products and spares. MRP II objectives will also usually include higher product quality; it represents a JIT philosophy of production and materials control.

JIT was developed initially in Japan and represents a comprehensive managerial philosophy based on customer service and requirements with idle resources eliminated throughout the company. Improved quality control is an important objective and therefore the philosophy extends beyond the company to its suppliers who need to supply quality-assured components if production schedules are to be met. JIT would ideally result in no components being held until they were required for production with orders being triggered by daily production requirements.

18 Mergers and acquisitions

Introduction

This chapter deals with the factors affecting corporate acquisitions. An acquisition occurs when one company acquires a controlling interest (i.e. over 50% of the voting capital) of another company. The most usual outcome is for the whole of the company to be acquired. The terms merger and takeover are used more or less synonymously in discussion on acquisitions. In general use takeovers are seen to be the situation when one company acquires and absorbs another company; on the other hand, mergers are viewed as the situation when two or more companies of approximately the same size combine together to form a larger business organization. There are technical definitions of mergers and takeovers contained in the regulations relating to the accounting treatment of business combinations.

Economic factors of mergers

Financial theory examined to date suggests that if markets are viewed as efficient then for a merger to be successful the value of the two companies after the merger must be greater than the sum of the two individual companies prior to the merger. If we are considering the merger of two companies X and Y then

$$PV_{XY} > PV_X + PV_Y$$

Unless there is this increase in present value of the merged organization over the sum of the individual values of the merging companies there is no economic rationale for a merger to take place. An umbrella term embracing a number of economic benefits of merging is referred to as synergy, that is the value of the combined organizations is worth more than the simple sum of the parts.

Mergers are sometimes classified under the following headings:

1. **Horizontal.** These are mergers between companies in a similar business activity and at the same stage of the production or distribution chain, e.g. Motor car manufacturers.

2. **Vertical.** These indicate mergers between companies in the same line of business but at different stages of the production and distribution chain, e.g. merger between a garment manufacturer and clothing retailer.
3. **Conglomerate.** This term is used to describe mergers between companies in unrelated lines of business, e.g. a tobacco company acquires companies in financial services and retailing industry.

Reasons for an increase in value arising on merger include the following:

1. Economies of scale are claimed as a major benefit. This is particularly so in the case of horizontal mergers, e.g. steel, chemical and automobile companies have formed large units to gain economies in production, marketing and research and development by spreading these costs over a larger sales and assets base. Such economies have also been claimed for conglomerate mergers (usually in areas of centralized management and services to management), but as we shall see, it is probably easier to buy a company than to integrate it into existing operations.
2. Management inefficiency. If the company is badly managed its assets may not be fully utilized. Markets will place a lower value on these companies than better managed similar companies. The inefficient companies will therefore be vulnerable to takeover by managers of other companies who will be able to justify paying a price higher than market value because they have confidence in their ability to eliminate inefficiencies and earn a higher return than that currently being obtained from the assets of the company. In these circumstances, mergers can be represented as useful to all parties concerned except the inefficient management! Management is unlikely to fire itself, owners (shareholders) are likely to be too fragmented and unorganized to fire them, so takeover could therefore benefit shareholders in both bidding and target company.

Financial aspects

Attempts are sometimes made to distinguish between a merger and a takeover. As both result in the combination of previously separate business entities the distinction is not important except in certain specific circumstances. One specific area of importance is in methods of accounting for business combinations. For accounting purposes the combined business may be treated either on a merger or acquisition basis. The advantages of merger accounting as opposed to acquisition accounting include the allowance of pre-acquisition profits of both companies to remain available for distribution to shareholders; assets do not have to be written up to their fair market value; and goodwill and share premium accounts do not have to be opened. On the other hand, acquisition accounting requires the pre-acquisition profits of acquired companies to be capitalized and therefore not available for distribution. In addition, assets of acquired companies have to be written up to their fair market value and goodwill and share premium accounts opened. It is possible therefore for companies using the merger method to show accounting results that appear superior to those prepared under the acquisition method.

However, it should be emphasized that this is really another cosmetic difference as the method of accounting will not change the economic reality of the business being carried on.

The main conditions which the Companies Act 1989 states for a combination to be regarded as a merger are that

1. One company has secured at least 90% of the shares carrying unrestricted participation rights.
2. The shares were obtained by an exchange of equity shares in the parent company or one of its subsidiaries.
3. The fair value of any other consideration was not more than 10% of the value of the equity shares issued.
4. Prior holdings in the acquired company must not exceed 20% of the total shares in that company.

In addition to the Companies Act definition there is an Accounting Standard which seeks to define a merger and sets out conditions which must be satisfied before merger accounting is permitted. If the conditions in the Act and the Accounting Standards are met, merger accounting is permitted but not compulsory.

Another accounting aspect of mergers and takeovers is the role P/E ratios have played in justifying merger terms. The strategy adopted is for a company with a high P/E ratio to acquire companies with a lower P/E ratio. The combination would result in an immediate increase in earnings per share which if capitalized at the existing P/E ratio of the acquiring company, as has sometimes been the case, would result in an enhanced share price. An example is given below showing how this strategy would operate.

Increasing EPS by takeover

	Yuppy plc	*Staid plc*	*Yuppy after acquiring Staid*
EPS	20p	20p	26.7p
Share price	£4	£2	£4
P/E ratio	20	10	15
No. of shares	1 000 000	1 000 000	1 500 000
Total earnings	£200 000	£200 000	£400 000
Total market value	£4 000 000	£2 000 000	£6 000 000

Yuppy takes over Staid by issuing one new share for every two of Staid in line with market values. Yuppy with high anticipated growth buys Staid with low anticipated growth and, assuming no additional economic benefits, column three shows situation which should occur. Effectively, Yuppy shareholders forgo some growth to Staid shareholders in exchange for an immediate increase in EPS and perhaps dividend.

However, in a number of instances investors have assumed or have been pursuaded that the high growth P/E rating should apply to the enlarged organization. In this case if a P/E of 20 was applied to the combined business a value of $-26.7p \times 20 = £5.34$ would arise. In fact any rating higher than 15 would have the effect of instantly increasing the wealth of both sets of shareholders!

The example shows the adjustment in P/E ratio and price that should take place when the merger occurs. If there are no identifiable economic advantages of merging then the value of the two firms after merger should merely be the sum of the two individual companies prior to merging. The nub of the problem is that high P/E ratios indicate high anticipated levels of growth while lower P/E ratios indicate lower growth, or maybe in certain circumstances a steady state with no growth. When the two business organizations are combined one would expect the growth rate and hence P/E ratio of the combined business to be at an appropriately lower figure.

Tax advantages can sometimes accrue on a takeover. The target company may have accumulated tax allowances it is unable to use. If this unused tax shield can be used by the acquiring company it obviously has a value. However, care must be exercised in using this as a motive for acquisition because the tax carryover is not automatic.

Risk diversification
Diversification of risk is sometimes suggested as a factor in merger activity. Initially it may seem to make sense, for example, for a tobacco company to acquire companies in other business activities. However, investors are perfectly capable of carrying out this diversification for themselves (and will be assumed to have done so) and if companies do this there may in fact be a transfer of wealth to debt holders through the co-insurance effect provided by uncorrelated income flows jointly, guaranteeing interest and repayment of debt.

Management motives
It is the managers of companies who initiate and defend takeover bids and although in either case they should be seeking to maximize shareholder returns it has been suggested that it would be possible for them to pursue policies which are perceived to be in their own best interest.

Managers' pay, reputation and status are likely to be greater the larger the organization, thus encouraging takeover/merger activity. From a manager's point of view risk diversification might be considered a good thing and encourage conglomerate takeovers. On the other hand, managers of acquired companies are likely to lose their jobs and this could lead them to resist takeovers on behalf of shareholders, even though these takeovers may be in the best financial interest of shareholders.

This potential conflict of interest has been recognized in a number of ways, e.g. where contracts called 'Golden Parachutes' are given to managers awarding generous compensation if they are displaced on takeover.

Methods of payment

The consideration for the acquisition may be either in cash, shares or debt, or some combination of cash and 'paper'.

Target company shareholders may prefer cash because

1. It fixes the price they will receive and removes the uncertainty of market quotations which a share for share exchange would bring.
2. Their liquidity is increased and they are in a position to diversify their portfolio.

On the other hand, there are disadvantages. An individual shareholder becomes immediately liable to pay capital gains tax on any gain arising. This does not happen in a share-for-share exchange because the shares received are regarded as replacing those in the acquired company. However, it should be noted that the tax position of institutional shareholders is different. Investment trusts, unit trusts and pension funds are exempt from capital gains tax, although insurance companies are still liable for this tax.

The bidding company might prefer to offer cash because

1. It is easily understood by the shareholders of the victim company as it does not vary from day to day with market conditions.
2. The cash offer does not result in the issue of additional shares and therefore the bidding company shareholders will retain their control over the resulting larger organization.

In the case of non-quoted companies, acquisitions will invariably be for cash, the lack of marketability virtually ruling out a share offer.

Target company shareholders may prefer a share-for-share exchange as consideration because

1. Capital gains tax is deferred.
2. Shareholders still retain a financial interest in the company they have sold.

However, there are disadvantages for major shareholders in target companies who may end up having a very large proportion of their total wealth invested in a single company. Realization through the market may not always be a practical possibility due to the effect sales of large numbers of shares may have on the quoted price.

From the point of view of the bidding company, the issue of a large number of further shares may alter the power structure of the company.

The bidding company's cash flow benefits with a share-for-share exchange. No cash is paid out for the initial acquisition and dividend payments on additional shares issued may well be lower than the equivalent debt in the early years following the merger.

Fixed interest securities and convertibles have at times been used as consideration in mergers. A significant problem in recent years has been fixing a coupon rate attractive to target company shareholders without being excessively high from the point of view of the bidding company. Packages of loan stock and convertibles can be used as consideration but a number of convertibles have not lived up to expectations and shareholders and their advisors are now much more wary about this type of consideration. Convertibles can also carry the right to be repaid at a premium as an alternative to conversion, should the share price be lower than hoped. However, this can add significantly to the cost of issuing convertibles and place a strain on company resources, often when the company is least able to cope with extra cash payments.

Takeover tactics

Bidding company tactics
Having identified a suitable acquisition the purchasing company must decide how to conduct its takeover. The objective will be to make the offer as attractive as possible to the victim company shareholders at the least possible cost to the purchasing company. The existing stock market price of a quoted victim company will generally set the lower limit to the price which will have to be paid. This emphasizes the need to identify economic benefits of merger prior to making the bid. If markets are assumed to be efficient, then the prices will already reflect a consensus view of the value of the target company and therefore sound reasons for merging need to be identified to justify paying a price higher than current market value.

Takeover bidders will have to operate within the regulations of the Companies Act 1989 and also the City Code on takeovers and mergers. The latter Code is part of the self regulatory machinery under which the City operates and is issued on the authority of the Council for the Securities Industry.

The Companies Act disclosure requirements are that any person who acquires an interest in 5% or more of the voting share capital of a listed company must notify the company within five days of acquiring the interest. However, problems can still arise, particularly with dawn raids and concert parties.

Dawn raids occur when a person or company acts with great speed in buying the shares of a target company so that they achieve their objective before being required to notify the company of the acquisition. Typically these raids take place in the minutes or hours immediately after the stock market is open. These raids can bid up the price of the shares and it is obviously inequitable if only larger institutional shareholders in touch with the market benefit and small shareholders cannot obtain the same terms. The City Code has been strengthened so that all shareholders have to be made the same offer. The offer price cannot be less than the highest price paid for the shares within the preceding 12 months.

Concert parties describes the action where several persons act in concert to buy shares in a particular company in such a way that no one owns more than 5% and so is not liable to notify the target company. This loophole has now been closed and disclosure requirements now extend to such groups.

The company intending to bid must tell the Board of the victim company or their advisors, who then inform the shareholders. The bidder must disclose the terms of the bid and the identity of the bidders. Initially the offer is conditional and must remain open for 21 days. The offer becomes unconditional when the offeror gets acceptance for more than 50% of the capital. Up to the point where the offer becomes unconditional shareholders in the target company are able to change their mind about acceptance, but once the offer becomes unconditional this option is no longer available to them.

Target company tactics

Directors of a company subject to a takeover bid should seek to act in the best interests of the shareholders. They should seek independent advice when a bid is received. Recommendations to reject the bid could be based on the premise that either (a) the value of the offeror's shares is too high, or (b) the value of the target company's shares is too low. Both these defences beg the question of market efficiency but in the case of (b) the target company's directors could justify their claim by providing further information that perhaps is only available to them. If indeed under-valuation is claimed, then the following steps will usually be taken:

1. Assets will be revalued.
2. Revised profit forecasts will be issued.
3. Future dividends may well be forecast at higher levels than currently anticipated by the market.
4. Changes may be announced to improve efficiency and profitability.

The City Code requires defensive circulars to be prepared with the same care as if a Companies Act prospectus was being prepared.

A number of exotically named strategies have evolved for defending takeover bids. A target company may seek a takeover from another company which is seen as friendlier and more sympathetic to the aims of the target, the friendly acquirer is referred to as a white knight.

Poison pill strategies are those where the target makes itself less attractive to potential bidders. One method is for existing shareholders to be given options to buy loan stock or preference shares. If a bid is made before the options can be exercised the rights are automatically converted into ordinary shares. These shares will have to be purchased by the bidder adding to the acquisition cost.

Golden parachutes may be held by target management giving them substantial payments if the company is acquired. This may add substantially to the cost of acquisition. From shareholders' viewpoint this may (a) encourage management to accept profitable approach rather than defending their own interests, or (b) encourage them to accept *any* approach if the parachute is too golden.

Benefits of mergers

There has been considerable discussion and some empirical work on the parties that benefit from merger. Possible gainers or losers would include the economy (the social gain), shareholders of the bidding firm, shareholders of the target firm, directors of the bidding firm, directors of the target firm, employees of the two firms and financial institutions involved in the acquisition.

1. Social gains — a number of studies have tried to evaluate the impact of mergers and takeovers on the economy as a whole. There are implications here for public policy. The general results are disappointing

for the economy as a whole. The general thrust of the evidence suggests that on average any gains in efficiency are small and offset by potential social costs generated by increased market power created by larger organizations.

2. Gains to shareholders — the weight of evidence indicates that it is the shareholders of the victim company who make substantial gains. The average gain made by the bidding company shareholders is very much lower. A suggested reason for this could be that the bidding company has to pitch its initial offer above the victim company's current market value and if the bid is defended initially the final price paid may have to be substantially above the original offer.

3. Directors of the bidding firm — there is general agreement that the directors of the bidding firm benefit from a successful acquisition. They acquire increased status and power and there is evidence that they also receive increased financial rewards.

4. Directors of the victim firm — little evidence exists on the effect to this group. They are likely to lose if only because they are likely to be dismissed. However, it is usual for directors to have a service agreement and if so they could receive a substantial 'golden handshake'. In addition, if they are shareholders in the firm, evidence suggests that they will be gainers.

5. Employees — not a great deal of empirical evidence exists on the effect on employees. However, many mergers involve rationalization of production and other areas and it is possible that some employees will lose their jobs.

6. Financial institutions — advisors on takeovers, merchant bankers, public relation firms, etc., will be engaged by both sides in a merger situation. These professionals are therefore in a winning situation; their fees will have to be paid whatever the outcome of the offer.

Factors for success or failure in mergers

Evidence suggests that a significant proportion of mergers prove to be unsuccessful, e.g. Kitching's study in the USA concluded that three out of four mergers fail. A particularly high rate of failure was identified in conglomerate mergers, with vertical and horizontal mergers usually proving more successful. These studies stress that synergy does not automatically arise. Opportunities may be there, but the success of the merger depends upon management's ability to realize potential economies. Quality of management and having managers who can handle change are seen to be vital for success.

Valuation of companies

The acquisition of a company can be treated as any other investment appraisal by comparing the benefits to be derived in the future with the cost of acquiring those benefits. However, in that the project comprises the purchase of an entire business undertaking, it is likely to be on a much larger scale than normal projects.

The major problem lies in determining the value of future benefits to be derived. Although use is often made of data relating to past profits or dividends and historic cost or current value of assets, it must always be borne in mind that *future expected* profits and values should determine what we are prepared to pay now for the business.

The final price to be paid will be settled by negotiation. The purchasing company will have a maximum price it is prepared to pay while the vendors are likely to have a minimum acceptable price. In the case of quoted companies the minimum price will usually be related to the current quoted price.

The approaches to valuation can be summarized under the following headings:

(a) Present value of future receipts
This is classic investment appraisal and says that:

Value = PV of incremental cash flows to be derived from acquisition

Although this is theoretically sound it requires a forecast of all future cash flows relating to the acquisition. Information may not be available to make these forecasts and this is why analysts tend to use the more 'rule of thumb' capitalization of earnings. Because of the sensitivity of the PV method to the discount rate used, Stapleton suggested that the analyst should start by considering the current market value of the company to be acquired and then add to this the PV of the benefits expected to arise from the acquisition. This has the advantage of concentrating the mind on the evaluation of the additional benefits to be derived. If financial markets are efficient then there must be expected synergy or the acquisition will not be worthwhile.

(b) Capitalization of earnings
This approach capitalizes a projected earnings figure, often based on historic figures after making allowance for changes arising on acquisition. It should be noted that the earnings yield and P/E approach are variants of the same technique, the P/E ratio being the reciprocal of the earnings yield.

This is an easy tool to employ but relies on the estimation and maintenance of future profits and on the use of appropriate rates of return or P/E ratios. Industry sector average rates and P/Es are often more reliable than individual company figures.

Value = P/E Ratio × Total projected earnings

(c) Asset valuation
Asset values may be used where earnings figures are regarded as unreliable and/or unpredictable. Balance sheet values based on historic cost may not be regarded as suitable for valuation purposes. Two asset values, at least, can be considered:

1. break-up or liquidation value — this is normally regarded as a minimum value;
2. current value — current cost of assets to be used in business as going concern.

(d)   Some combination of (b) and (c)

Other methods involve valuation of assets plus a goodwill valuation which may be based on the accepted custom and usage of the business concerned and relates to the superior earning capacity of the business.

Although the PV method is theoretically superior, the other methods are more common in practice. The analyst may well use both earnings and asset approaches to reach a negotiating position. The initial starting point will be dependent on whether the analyst is acting for buyer or seller. Both will have an initial starting point with negotiation limits.

Company restructuring

In recent years a number of strategies have emerged whereby companies have sought to increase the benefits of shareholders by changing the asset structure of the group or the way in which the assets are owned. Among these are the following.

Disinvestment

This entails selling off part or parts of the company business. This could be viewed as the reverse of diversification and like diversification, in theory, disposing of parts of the business should not add to the overall value of the firm. However, it is quite possible that certain groups of assets may be managed more profitably by one set of managers than another. Perhaps there are particular business activities which are regarded as incompatible with the main business undertaken by the company; or it may be felt that particular activities are taking up too much valuable management time and that the overall business would benefit from a sale of these activities. Disinvestment may also be undertaken where a company is short of cash or wishes to improve its reported profits by selling a loss making activity. Where disinvestment involves selling to a third party it is termed a **sell-off**.

Alternatively the managers of a division may be invited or they may offer to buy the unwanted business from the company. In the 1980s the number of **management buy-outs** grew rapidly. The buy-outs were often highly levered with managers also borrowing to buy equity. With rising stock markets some fortunes were made when companies bought out were floated on the USM, but with a downturn in the market some buy-outs have found themselves in difficulties because of high leverage combined with high interest rates. It is felt by some that managers and workers will more closely identify with a company that they have a substantial investment in. On the other hand, there are potential conflicts of interest where managers may use privileged knowledge about the company to negotiate a buy out.

Spin-off

This occurs when shareholders in a group are given shares in individual companies in the group. There is no change in overall ownership, only in the form it takes. By separating operating units into autonomous, self-reporting companies it is hoped that the overall value of the group will increase. This is the reverse of the synergistic effects sometimes claimed for mergers and more in line with the 'small is beautiful' view of company size. It is hoped that the management and workforce of companies spun off will feel a greater sense of identification with the smaller unit of organization and thus feel more strongly motivated. The stock market dealers may also find it easier to value companies in this split-off form and thus the overall value of investors holdings may rise.

Going private

A number of individuals or a single wealthy individual may purchase all the shares of a public company, thus reverting to private company status. The purchasers will often be the original owners or their family prior to the initial public listing of the company. An example of this strategy occurred when Richard Branson, the founder, bought back Virgin Company shares from institutional and private shareholders. Branson had previously built the company up and sold shares to the public, thus obtaining a public listing.

Reasons for going private include:

1. Former sole or family owners wish to regain the independence previously enjoyed in private company status. It may be felt that they face current or potential interference in decision making from substantial outside shareholders.
2. The potential threat of takeover is eliminated. Although markets are widely regarded as being semi-strong form efficient anomalies, e.g. small companies, have been identified. Managers may believe that the market is undervaluing the company in the short term and this may cause them to decide to go private.
3. The administrative burden and costs complying with listing requirements will be eliminated.

Buy-in

In a buy-in a team of external, experienced managers seek to gain control of a group of assets, company or operating division. In essence it is a 'mini-takeover' from outside and may be contrasted with buy-outs which are initiated from within the company. The buy-in team will often be backed by a venture capitalist who will provide a mix of finance, often resulting in a highly geared position. Both the managers buying in and the venture capitalist will have equity stakes which they hope will provide substantial gains if, as is usually the intention, the company obtains a stock exchange listing.

Share repurchase

This strategy is discussed in Chapter 12 on dividend policy, p. 102.

References

Altman, E.I. (1968) Financial ratios, discriminant analysis and the prediction of corporate bankrupcy. *Journal of Finance*, September.

Miller, M.H. (1977) Debt and Taxes, *Journal of Finance*, **32**, 261–76.

Miller, M.H. and Modigliani, F. (1961) Dividend policy, growth and the valuation of shares, *Journal of Business*, **34**, 411–33.

Modigliani, F. and Miller, M.H. (1958) The cost of capital, corporation finance and the theory of investment, American Economic Review, **38**, 261–96.

Modigliani, F. and Miller, M.H. (1963) Taxes and the cost of capital: a correction, American Economic Review, **53**, 433–43.

Stapleton, R.C. (1976) The acquisition decision as a capital budgeting problem. *Journal of Business Finance and Accounting*, **2**, (2).

Taffler, R.J. (1982) Forecasting company failure in the UK using discriminant analysis and financial ratio data. *Journal of the Royal Statistical Society*, Series A, **145**, (3), 342–58.

Index